INDIA'S WILD WONDERS

Tigers are solitary creatures and a tigress rears the cubs on her own.
This friendly tigress at the Kanha National Park allowed us to photograph
her family from close range. One of the three 8-week old cubs sits by her,
while the other two are hidden among rocks. Between intervals,
we photographed this family over two years.

A herd of wild elephants at the Corbett National Park,
one of the most beautiful reserves in India. The jumbo has a keen
sense of smell and is sharp of hearing. Some of the herd raise their trunks
in periscopic fashion, to smell us out.

A column of Tibetan wild ass, *kiang*, crossing the Chang-thang plateau.
The ass has adapted itself to the extreme climatic fluctuations of the arctic-desert of
Ladakh. *Kiang* herds migrate between India and Tibet
and their numbers are growing in Ladakh.

A blue bull in full gallop in the Rann of Katch. It can run at impressive speeds over uneven surfaces. Indians, who call it *nilgai*, feel it is related to the holy cow and will not hunt it. Blue bulls are found in most scrub-forest biotopes in India but do not occur extralimitally.

Copyright © 1994 Rajesh Bedi/Naresh Bedi
Original edition published in 1991
by Brijbasi Printers Private Limited, New Delhi, India

This edition published by Euredition bv,
Luiksestraat 23, 2587 AL The Hague, Netherlands

Produced by Euredition bv, Den Haag, Netherlands

Designed by Gopi Gajwani

Phototypeset by Alphabets

Printed and bound in Singapore

ISBN 90-75082-01-0

INDIA'S WILD WONDERS

Photographs by
RAJESH BEDI

Text by
NARESH BEDI

A Himalayan black bear stripping the bark from a sissoo tree in the foothills.
It is found along the great Himalayan range, Kashmir and Assam.
The other bear widely distributed in India is the sloth bear.
For this photograph Rajesh Bedi won the Photographer of the Year Award 1986,
in an international wildlife competition held in U.K.

The Call of the Jungle

At four o'clock in the afternoon, I started on my return journey from the lake's southern end, with a camera assistant and one of our local trackers. At 4572 m, in May the Tso Morari – one of Ladakh's unusual landlocked, salt-water lakes – was still largely frozen. The southern end of the lake was a haphazard heap of ice packs, rumbling to the waters underneath. The expanse of the gigantic lake reduced to insignificance the speed of our inflatable boat and in a bid to rev up the engine we had jammed the system. That set us back by half an hour and the gathering force of the northwesterly wind pushed the boat back to the ice floe on the edge of the lake. Our investigative probe had been in vain. Not a single bar-headed goose was to be seen. The island on the southeast was supposed to be full of nests. It was not to be seen either; probably buried under a thick coat of snow and quite untraceable in that frozen section of the lake. By the time we began moving again, the high wind had turned the lake into a stormy sea. Waves four feet high and seething with foam tossed the dinghy about and as I held on to the throttle, the boys began bailing water out with the help of the thermos cap and cup. We were in the centre of the lake and the boys wanted me to try and cut to the western shore. But because of the rocks I knew we stood no chance there against the raging water. There was only one way out, to risk riding the waves and make the long journey to the north. We had spent only ten days at the Tso Morari and had no idea of its tidal fury, late in the afternoon when a strong wind cut over Karzok village and threw the lake into turmoil. The waves would toss the boat up in the air from time to time, the outboard engine would stop and we would have to restart it. Somehow we managed to push on. I knew our direction was right. I could see the hill below which we had set up our camp, but I also saw the sun setting behind the hills. It became darker and darker. The chill water of the lake had swamped the dinghy. My hands, holding on to the engine's throttle, were numb. For the first time in twenty-two years of wildlife filming, I feared I would not make it home.

It seemed as though we would be defeated by the lake. Tso Morari, 23.3 km from north to south, a wedge of brackish water 6 km. broad cordoned by steep and barren hills. The first rays of summer had opened up an oblong strip of water in the lake. A jagged ribbon of ice ran along the lake's length. I had ventured that afternoon to probe the unfamiliar southern section. Villagers at Karzok, on the lake's northern extremity where we had set up camp, had pointed to a spot to the south where a large colony of bar-headed geese bred. Rajesh and I had set up a camouflage hide on one of the islands close to Karzok, but in mid-May there were only a handful of birds there. For over a year we had been planning to document the mating and breeding habits of the bar-headed goose. Little was known of this in reliable detail. Their nesting sites at Tso Morari are almost inaccessible during the breeding season. The lake is locked in the inner regions of the Chang-thang plateau, stretching west from Tibet behind the Great Himalayas. In spite of these apparent obstacles, Rajesh and I had been determined, for almost a year, to set up camp well in time to photograph the nesting of the birds and the hatching of their eggs. A hair-raising drive across the high passes and through four feet of water, in the partially frozen fresh-water inlets to the lake, had brought us to Karzok in May the previous year. One little island close to the village had come alive with a small population of bar-headed geese, some of whom had already made their nests.

Was there a larger colony of nests behind the jagged protrusion of the hill towards the south, as the Karzok villagers said? There was only one way to find out. I left Rajesh behind, to continue filming on the island, and sped in our rubber dinghy to explore the southern end of the lake. Though they live by it and steal the eggs of the geese, the villagers of Karzok do not have any kind of a relationship with the lake. It is cold right through the year and bathing is unknown among the villagers. The lake serves only as a watery grave and they cast their dead, in a sitting posture, into it, weighted by heavy stones; or leave them on the mountainside in winter, as there is no firewood in this barren country for a cremation. A boat seemed a novel contraption to the adults and something that the children had only read about in their school books. Nobody warned us, therefore, of the high tidal waves that roar across the lake in the afternoons and the danger these held for our rubber dinghy.

At the other end of the lake, around five o'clock, our cook waded to the island where Rajesh sat, to bring him back. As it turned out, it was not just my life that was in danger that afternoon. Carrying the cameras above their heads, Rajesh and the cook had to walk over thick, sticky mud through waist-deep water. The cook sank into a hole for a brief moment but managed to recover his step, the 16 mm Arriflex movie camera half submerged on his shoulder. Then, hardly three metres from the bank, Rajesh suddenly got stuck in the sticky mud up to his waist. The cold and the exhaustion caused by the thin, high-altitude air immobilized him temporarily. Rajesh felt so strained that he couldn't help himself at all. An intrepid, courageous young man, our cook Tashi, scurried back and forth, deposited his own and Rajesh's camera-load on the bank and pulled Rajesh out of the mud trap. It was past 5.30 p.m. and, as far as Rajesh knew, there was no sign of us on the turbulent waves of the lake. Accompanied by Tashi, he raced our jeep to a hillock along the western shore, but what he saw through the binoculars was a body being tossed about by the waves. The worst fears began to haunt him now: a body was visible, but where was the boat? It was not possible to drive beyond the hillock and we were not visible from where they scanned the lake. By then half the village had collected at our camp. Ominous stories began to be mumbled about the crocodilian-monster that lived in the depths of the Tso Morari, which would devour the three hapless passengers of the boat. Luckily, the 5 hp engine did not give way and around 8.30 p.m. our little dinghy finally crossed the silhouette of the hill atop which Rajesh stood in anxiety. With a torch I managed to flash

some kind of a signal. He focused the jeep's headlights upon the lake, counting us one by one, relieved that we were still together. Our feet had turned icy white and frosty in the water that had filled the bottom of the boat. The camera boxes were full of water, too, and we learnt later that five cameras were damaged beyond repair. Wearied and smitten by the cold, the boys no longer had the strength to bail the water out. I held on to the throttle for dear life and the brave little engine chugged on. We had survived being stalked by lions, man-eating tigers, elephant charges, crocodile nests, pythons and king cobras, and a dozen other predators of the jungle but the only time I feared certain death was on Tso Morari that fateful night.

We had been going into jungles and forests since we were three years old. I still remember being carried on my father's back through the forests in the Himalayan foothills. Father was a qualified doctor in Indian medicine. He worked at the forest-university of Gurukul Kangri, downstream from the ghats at Haridvar, in Uttar Pradesh. He had spent his childhood there and returned to it in 1947, after his family had lost their house and property at Lahore (now in Pakistan) during the Partition of India. We were fortunate in that we were born at Haridvar at the time we did. There is no doubt in my mind that my younger brother, Rajesh, and I would have turned to wildlife photography and filming no matter where we had been born, because of the tremendous inspiration we derived from the example of our father. Yet, being born at Haridvar was providential. Here we grew up at the edge of the Himalayan foothills and quickly imbibed from our father, one of the early conservationists in India, the captivating call of the wild.

Father's other love was animals. As he tramped through the forests in search of rare medicinal herbs, he developed a fond intimacy with the wild animals and a deep first-hand knowledge of their behaviour. Always curious, never deterred by the supposed dangers of the jungle, he could use a camera well and derived immense satisfaction from recounting his experiences in a continuous flow of articles on Indian wildlife that he published, along with these pictures, in mass-circulation Hindi magazines, though they paid him the proverbial tu'penny for his efforts. Yet, father couldn't care less. Perhaps, he simply wanted to share the excitement of his personal journeys through the forest. The wilds stirred him in a way the city never has.

At Haridvar we were within trekking distance of wild elephants. We saw tiger cubs for the first time when they followed their mother into a sugarcane field close to our house. There was a hornbill nesting site not more than thirty metres away and we would be fascinated every year by the way the male hornbill sealed the hole in the jamun tree where the female laid her eggs. The mother hornbill moults excessively after she lays eggs and is unable to fly. The male dexterously closes the tree hole with gum, mud, fibre and whatever else it can find, leaving open only a narrow slit through which it feeds the female. Inside the nest the female also uses her excreta to plaster the hole. As children we would hear stories every other day about small cats like the civet. Every time an animal was

spotted nearby, villagers and neighbours would rush to inform our father. If an orphaned little one had been seen, father would bring it home, giving it shelter and food till its confidence and strength was restored and it could traipse back to the forest. Animal life is noticeably interwoven with the fabric of the Indian's existence. As children, we would daily observe our mother worshipping Lord Shiva's bull, *Nandi*, and the snake wrapped around his neck, at the temple. The god Ganesha, with the elephant-head, is also worshipped in Hindu homes. Crocodiles and many of the birds are considered to be the sacred vehicles of diverse gods and godheads. Monkeys and langurs are regarded as the 'army' of Lord Hanuman. Householders regularly offer food to cows, ants and monkeys and feed fish at the ghats.

India's legacy of wild animals is the second largest in the world. There are about 350 species of mammals, 1200 species of birds and more than 20000 species of insect life to be found in India. The country's unique geographical location and divergent climatic conditions have bred an impressive diversity of wildlife.

Living with animals around the house made us fall in love with wildlife and taught us at a rather early stage the essentials about animal behaviour. After we shifted to the concrete maze of metropolitan Delhi, India's capital, father ensured that we spent at least one month of the summer vacation at the Corbett National Park, 290 km northeast of Delhi, part of the *terai* forest at the foothills of the Himalayas. India's first national park, it remains one of her finest. The tracts on either side of the river Ramaganga were popular hunting grounds which were converted, in 1935, into a game park inhabited by elephant, tiger, leopard, a variety of deer, wild boar, gharial, king cobra and diverse birds. The park was named in 1957 after the legendary Jim Corbett, huntsman-turned-author and wildlife photographer, whose books on the big cats are among the most exciting and authoritative accounts of their behaviour. We were both given our first still cameras before we had turned fifteen. Our childhood treks in and around Corbett Park taught us the value of having a strong pair of legs. We'd leave the park's resthouse early morning, carry a simple lunch and cover up to 30 kilometres a day.

We were following a herd of elephants in the Corbett once, because father wanted to observe its day's routine. We came to a bushy patch. Here, a female in the herd smelt us out. Alarmed, she turned and rushed towards us, but as she was charging through the long elephant grass a frightened peahen flew up from her feet and startled her. Confused, she forgot about us and went back to the herd. After we got over the shock of this sudden encounter, we took a longer and circuitous route, to a higher position than where we felt the elephants were heading. Here we were to observe and record the herd's activities and its young ones playing and jousting with each other. By the time we began our way back from the trek, the sun began to set. It is in the evenings that the nocturnal animals, like the big cats and bears, move out of their lairs and dens in search of food. On the way back we walked too

close to a sloth bear, the mother of two young cubs. They are known to have a ferocious temper and will attack without provocation. A bear with a young cub is most dangerous. But our tracker saved us that day. As soon as we saw the black bear at close range he asked us to scream and shout as loudly as we could and to pick up sticks. The trick worked that day, but each of us carried a stout staff in the hand all the way back to the resthouse. We arrived in the nick of time to stop an anxious forest officer from setting out with a search party for us.

I joined the course in cinematography at the Film & Television Institute of India, Pune, in 1967, because of my ambition to film India's rich and colourful wildlife. It perplexed all of us in the family that while film-makers and photographers from all over the world had focused extensively on the wildlife of Africa, Indian photographers failed to see the tremendous potential of documenting the immense diversity of animal life in India. But for the odd exception, our seniors in the profession had not thought of specialising in a study of Indian wildlife and among the film-makers there was nobody at all. The media did not offer much encouragement either. During his stint as a photographer with a leading daily newspaper at Delhi, Rajesh's offers of animal studies would be cursorily dismissed and at the office he was derided as the 'zoo photographer'. As a 16 mm cameraman, I was fortunate to get 30 second spots in the Sunday evening news bulletins of the Doordarshan TV station at Delhi, but these brief flashes about animal life were hardly enough. The writing on the wall seemed to say that we could not live by merely pursuing our first love. However this was not a state of affairs we were willing to accept. We knew that readers and viewers responded enthusiastically to our pictures, even if the news editors gave them a low priority.

A little later, *National Geographic* magazine asked us to do photographs of the *gharial*, the long-snouted, fish-eating crocodilian. They were doing a story on the crocodiles of the world but couldn't find any good pictures of the Ganges gharial. Till quite recently it, was to be found in rivers all over India, but the commercialized marauding of the twentieth century had brought it to the very brink of extinction. Rajesh and I had just started as freelancers and made do with a minimal amount of equipment. The *National Geographic* writer looked at Rajesh's camera bag and pointed out that he needed a long lens. We assured him we would get the pictures he wanted. All those weeks spent at the Corbett Park prompted us to believe that we could get close enough to photograph the gharial. Rajesh spent four weeks in search of gharials in different states giving a wide choice of pictures. During that period he also picked up a lot of information about the gharial that was yet undocumented and it inspired me to think of making my first independent wildlife documentary on the endangered reptile. This was to be our first independent venture and we aimed to make it in colour for the international market.

Indian film-makers, specially documentarists and among them wildlife film-makers even more so, suffer from a paucity of technical equipment available within the country. We com-

menced our film on the gharial with very basic equipment. What we had needed was a good camera, a long lens, a fluid-head tripod and lots of film stock at our disposal. We shot some rolls with what we had and got good material on film. We were hoping to interest some foreign TV networks, but we had still to prove ourselves. B.B.C s natural history unit was impressed by our material, but was not willing to fund our film, because they were uncertain whether we would be able to record the various activities of an elusive crocodilian that had become extremely rare and endangered. It was a very sad moment for the family, specially for father. But Rajesh and I were determined to carry on nevertheless. I was confident that we were on to a good film and we decided to go ahead with our project, whether anybody funded us or not. It took us five years to complete *The Ganges Gharial*, which is regarded by many as the finest film we have yet made. There are many firsts that the documentary offers and, for the two of us, it marks a definite breakthrough in Indian wildlife filming. I was happy to receive the Widescreen '84 Best Wildlife Camera Award. The film was shown on Channel 4 in U.K. and over PBS stations in USA and received very good reviews from the critics. Rajesh's photographs appeared in *National Geographic*. *Life* magazine published a special portfolio and many appeared in leading magazines elsewhere. With the success of the film we proved that we could deliver the goods and make wildlife films of international standard. The leading TV networks of the world, featuring wildlife films, began to show interest in our new projects and as wildlife photographers we had made the vital breakthrough.

Croc with a Hump on His Nose

The Ganges gharial *(Gavialis gan geticus)* takes its name from the *ghada* or the hump at the tip of the male's snout *(ghada* means a water-pot in Hindi). The hump resembles a pitcher; so gharial. A clerical mistake is actually responsible for giving it the name 'gavial' in natural history. It is the strangest and the most interesting of the crocodilians, a reptile that belongs to an ancient family that has existed for millions of years. At one time abundant throughout South Eastern Asia, it, was on the verge of extinction by 1969 when its numbers had reportedly shrunk to less than a hundred. It is one of the three crocodilian species to be found in India. The long narrow snout distinguishes it from the mugger *(Crocodylus palustris)* the marsh crocodile, and the estuarine or salt-water crocodile *(Crocodylus porosus)*. The gharial is a fish-eater and is regarded as harmless to man. A river-dweller, it is found in the water-systems of the Ganga, Brahmaputra and Mahanadi rivers. The peculiar jaws of the gharial, with 108 sharp teeth, are adapted to catching and manipulating fish under water. On catching fish, it will come to the surface and toss it into position before it swallows it, head first. This can take several minutes and if the fish is too large, the gharial will thrash its head from side to side above the water, breaking the fish into smaller pieces.

It was because of the *National Geographic* assignment that

Rajesh and I realized that in our wildlife studies we had to pay special attention to the species that were endangered. The gharial was our animal, an animal that was part of every Indian's experience till only recently, but by 1969 it had all but disappeared from the scene. Apart from the excesses of poaching, the industrial and demographic pressures and the consequent pollution of river waters had severely damaged the crocodilian's habitat. Filming its life-cycle for *The Ganges Gharial* was not easy. It took us five long years. Three were taken up in just filming the egg-laying sequences. For weeks together we would be drenched to the skin, alternately shivering or sweating in our airless camouflage-hide. Like the owl, we slept during the day and worked at night, when scorpions crawled over the sand and made life miserable for biped cameramen. Gharials are the most aquatic of the crocodilians and their front legs are poorly developed. This puts them to great disadvantage on land and they never venture far from the water's edge, so that they can return quickly to safety if necessary. They sleep for short periods, but are constantly listening for danger. The female crocodilian lays its eggs and hatches them always at night, because in the dark there is less danger from the predators like pigs and monitor lizards and humans are not to be seen. In the recent past a major threat to the regeneration of the species had been the theft of eggs by village folk along the Chambal and Mahanadi rivers, for whom gharial egg omlettes were a delicacy. On filming a gharial basking at Corbett, I even saw male otter biting the massive crocodilian's tail. The gharial quickly moved towards the otter mouth wide open, but the otter slipped away in the water to rejoin its companions.

The ravines of the Chambal river are infested with bandits. It is unsafe country. We had been advised to buy the protection of an ex-dacoit, who would also work as our guide, but this did not completely quell our fears. Could he really be trusted or would we be betrayed in the end? We could never be certain about his real intentions. But other dangers lurked in the nearby ravines. Word had evidently got around that a film unit was shooting by the Chambal. The very mention of a film unit conjures images of glamorous stars and movie mughals in the mind of the average Indian, who does not have a clue about the realities, the interests or the concerns of a documentarist. One evening we were attacked by a gang of young marauders, small-time bandits armed with lethal staffs. Our technical consultant was the first to see them and shouted at us to run. Rajesh and I dumped the camera in our boat and ran as fast as we could over the sand, disappearing in the dark. Our boatmen reacted instinctively. They took the boats into the river, hoping that the bandits would not enter the gharial-infested water. That saved our expensive equipment from being noticed by the bandits who would certainly have looted whatever they could lay their hands on. The project officer displayed exemplary courage. He was known locally as the fellow working on the gharial rehabilitation project. The bandits interrogated him about us, but accepted his statement that we were not glamorous film directors from Bombay; only naturalists interested in the laying and hatching of gharial eggs. They went off, in search of other prey. At the end, however, the two of us felt duly rewarded for our efforts. We were the first to film female gharials laying eggs and to capture the captivating relationship between the baby crocodilians and their parents.

Gharials mate in winter between December-January. The male emits a combination of whistles and hisses that are amplified by his nasal hum. It is a noise that can be compared only with the sound produced by a steam locomotive. Rajesh has made several recordings, by planting a hidden radio microphone at the spot favoured by the dominant male. A responsive female approaches the male, raises her snout besides him and responds with softer calls. Bubbling of air by both further confirms their acceptance of each other. Alternately surfacing and submerging, the partners then swim side by side towards shallow water where the male can mount her. After several attempts he got a secure hold on the female, then love-locked pair went down into the deep water to mate. When mating is over, the female moves away and the male may well entice another member to his harem. Contrary to the belief of many experts, the male does not use his hump as a hook while mounting the female. The hump is an indication of male's adulthood. Male hatchlings are not born with it. It begins to grow only after 10 years and we noticed that bigger males have bigger humps. A month after mating, the pregnant female climbs onto the river bank to search for a suitable nesting site. A gharial will lay her eggs on a sand bank close to the water and she digs a suitable nest, using her back legs to scoop out the sand. It can take as long as three hours to complete the digging. When the nest is deep enough, she begins to lay her eggs, at intervals of a minute and a half. She keeps her legs inside the nest to prevent damage from too great a fall. By the time the last egg has been laid, the female is clearly tired. But before returning to the water she will fill the hole with sand. It was three hundred million years ago that the reptiles developed an eggshell that could incubate outside water. This enabled them to conquer the land and they then dominated it for 200 million years. The crocodilians are aquatic leftovers from the time when reptiles ruled the world, the age of the dinosaurs. In fact, the gharial's whole nesting process is somehow highly reminiscent of that ancient age.

Many facts are still being discovered about the gharial's breeding habits. For example, a female gharial buries her eggs a foot below the surface. This is for a very good reason. Even when the surface of the sand becomes scorching hot, the eggs buried below remain at a uniform temperature of 30 to 35 degrees centigrade. This also protects them from predators. The mother vigilantly guards the nest from close by. After about 70 days, using the egg tooth at the end of its snout, the baby crocodilian will break the eggshell and begin to call. In response to the call of hatchlings, the female digs them out. This is a task she will perform by herself, chasing away the male if it strays too close to the nest. When the sand has been cleared, the hatchlings get their first lungful of air. The mother

will dig out her entire brood of 30 centimetre long babies. Many crocodile species carry their young to the water in their mouths, but gharials cannot do this because their teeth are too sharp and also because the position of their eyes would make it difficult for them to see the young inside the mouth. At one time people thought that gharials carried their young on their backs to the water, but it was not true in this case. The female excavate the nest in such a way that the hatchlings could come out and walk down to the water by themselves; the hatching process takes place over several hours. While the young are only a few weeks old the monsoon reaches its peak and the rivers become rushing torrents. Many hatchlings are swept away and only one per cent of them survive the crucial first weeks, as many fall prey to large fishes, turtles and birds.

The two other Indian crocodilians, the mugger and the salt-water crocodile happen to look similar, but they are to be found in different habitats. Muggers inhabit rivers, lakes and other large water bodies and are found up to 600 m in the hills, throughout the subcontinent. The salt-water crocodile inhabits the tidal estuaries of the larger rivers, the mangrove swamps and the coastal backwaters. Both species are endangered and are protected by law.

The crocodile is a picture of grace and elegance in the water, but we also happened to be witness to the crocodile's ferocity in an unusually dramatic sequence at the Ranthambore National Park in Rajasthan. Driving down a dirty track near the lake, we were jolted by the sight of a group of muggers which had encircled the carcass of a full-grown spotted deer quite far from water. Strutting aggressively on their dwarfed feet, their armoured backs swollen, they seemed like prehistoric reptiles as they tried to rip open the carcass, holding it with their teeth and turning savagely to tear the skin. Disturbed by our intrusion, the muggers fled into the lake, but it was not long before a big fellow came out of the water and pulled the dead deer in. Before he took it down with him he rose above the water with a heave, twirled the carcass in an incredibly fast spin to break open the skin and then disappeared underwater. It was an amazing scene.

The first crocodile-breeding project in India started in 1975 in Orissa. Since then several rehabilitation, protection and conservation projects have come up in some other states, too. The aim of crocodile-breeding projects is to collect eggs from crocodile nests, hatch these and rear the young at the rehabilitation centres. And after they reach a certain maturity of age, to release the young in specially protected river-zones. Thousands of gharials and muggers have been reared by the various breeding centres and have reached a level where they are no longer an endangered species. What further needs to be attended to is the restoration of their breeding grounds, so that they start breeding in their natural habitat.

Sher : The Legendary Tiger

To see a tiger in the wild is one of the most thrilling experiences nature has to offer. It is the biggest of the big cats and is charismatically handsome : powerful, beautiful to look at and a symbol of strength. The tiger figures prominently in our folklore and has a special status in our history, mythology and religion. Numbers dramatically decreased, due to excessive hunts during the last hundred years, from an estimated 40-50000 at the turn of the century to a mere 1827 in 1972. But from 1973, Project Tiger has considerably restored some of the lost numbers and the tiger population in India is now estimated to be around 4500, as per the 1990 census. We spotted our first tiger at Corbett in the early seventies, almost ten years after we began visiting the park. We were sitting patiently on a machan when we heard the cheetal and peacock alarm calls. A little later, a tigress strolled up to the artificial waterhole near the machan. Then, it signalled to the two cubs hiding in the bush. The cubs played in the water for about twenty or twenty-five minutes before the family returned to the forest.

Jim Corbett, legendary huntsman-turned-conservationist and father-figure to Indian wildlife-lovers, felt that the best and most honourable way of hunting the tiger was on foot, in a one to one equation. But for the photographer or the cameraman that is not the best way to 'shoot' a tiger. Trained riding elephants are extremely helpful in tiger-spotting. Tigers move over a fairly vast territory and do not have regular haunts, where a cameraman could fruitfully wait for the striped beauty. Much of the Indian tiger's activity takes place behind the veil of tall jungle grass or within dense foliage, where it is dangerous to be on foot. A much closer access to the tiger is possible on trained riding elephants whose presence in the forest is familiar to tigers and the other animals. Though the elephant is a somewhat timid giant, very few predators will charge at it because of its size. Elephants can negotiate the difficult terrain of the tiger's habitat more comfortably than any other mode of conveyance.

However, the elephant's back is not the surest of positions that a film cameraman can take, because the elephant is an animal which is never still, even when it's standing at one spot. It becomes difficult, therefore, to take a steady picture. So, when we went to the Kanha National Park to film *Saving the Tiger,* on the animal's behaviour and the conservation efforts, Rajesh and I put together in 1986 a special 2.80 metre high tripod with a revolving seat for the cameraman. Initially, there was a lot of scepticism expressed whether our elongated tripod would work, but it turned out to be a great device. The concept behind the mechanism was simple. When we had tracked down a tiger from an elephant's back, the three legs of the camera stand would be stretched down to the ground and whoever was filming would sit on the tripod's small, revolving seat, which would be at such a height as to give an impression to the tiger that one still sat on top of the elephant. The elephant would carefully be moved a step behind the tripod, however, so that it did not disturb the tripod's legs. It proved most useful and helped us to film rare behaviour of a tigress and her very young cubs.

This tigress turned out to be extremely co-operative from our point of view. It took us a good fifteen days to find her, after we first heard that a tigress with three new-born cubs had

been seen in the vicinity. We would go out daily with a caravan of three or four elephants early in the morning in search of her, in the territory where she was known to hunt. Having additional elephants helped to cover a larger area and we'd be looking for signs of tiger presence like alarm calls, and fresh pug marks on the jungle tracks and nullahs. All to no avail. Then suddenly one day we found the cubs on top of a hillock. They looked like small bundles of fur, hardly able to stand on their tiny legs. They seemed to be ten days old and their eyes had just opened. The place was rocky, with a bamboo cluster and there was only one point from which we could see the cubs. We placed the tripod on the slippery rock and sent the other elephants back, so that their presence did not disturb the tigress. A little later we saw her coming round a rock projection. She purred and called as she moved close to the cubs, then turned her eyes towards us and stared for a few seconds. We were only nine metres away, but neither the elephant nor my elongated tripod caused her any alarm. She was familiar with it, for I had filmed her on an earlier occasion. She was very confident and a big, beautiful tigress, the first with a litter that we learnt about, after a year's enquiry at the Kanha National Park. The cubs woke up at hearing her low purr, and the tigress picked up a cub in her mouth and turned towards the camera. It was a perfect shot, something I had always wanted to film. For a minute or so she held the cub, purring all the while, wondering whether she should move away or not. Then she changed her mind, put the cub down on the ground and sat next to it. The three cubs moved in to suckle at her teats. Suddenly, there emerged yet another, larger, cub. This one was a year old and looked weak and under-developed for his age. He shoved the little ones aside and took first share of mother's milk. This was most unusual. Unlike most tigresses, who come in oestrus only after an interval of two to three years, this one seemed to have conceived in two consecutive years and a weak cub from the previous litter was still very dependent on his mother.

The new-born cubs seemed to doze off while suckling. When the mother felt that they had drunk their fill, she got up, yawned, and carefully picked up a cub in her mouth, holding it behind the canines. She held it gently and, because it was now well-fed, it slept undisturbed as the mother carefully and adroitly shifted the cub around to get a proper grip. One by one she took the three cubs behind the hillock to our left. As she made her journeys back and forth, the older cub stayed behind, presumably guarding its half-brothers, till the mother had moved them all to a safer haven. Later we discovered that there was a sheer drop on the other side and that she had taken the cubs to a cave right behind the spot where we had filmed them. For the next fortnight we failed to see them again.

We saw somebody else instead, her one year old cub. It was drizzling, the cub lay whining on its back. The whining scared the elephant, which wouldn't budge closer than six metres of the prostrate cub, even though this one was known to be an extremely sturdy and calm animal. Some riding elephants are so scared of the tiger that as soon as they smell the striped cat,

even if it has merely passed that way through the tall grass, they will bang their trunk against the ground in alarm. A good look at the cub revealed that he was very very sick and so weak that the bones stuck out. Flies swarmed over him and he was in urgent need of medical help. We sent back one of the elephants so that the mahout could inform the Kanha director and give us permission to bring the cub for treatment. The permission was not the problem. None of the forest guards accompanying us wanted to pick up the sick cub; such is the fear of the tiger. We started by checking the area thoroughly, making sure that the cub's mother wasn't around to disturb the rescue operation. Once we were assured on that score, we got down from the elephant. I tried to give it milk from a bottle, but it refused to drink. Everybody soon realized that it was in a totally helpless state. We forced an elephant to sit on its knees, picked up the cub and lay it on the howdah. The cub was in great pain and offered no resistance at all. It had a gaping wound in a hind leg which was full of maggots. As we were returning to the resthouse, the drizzle turned into a terrible torrent which simply wouldn't stop. The whole area was soon flooded. Luckily, we were carrying huge tarpaulin sheets with us, to protect the howdah's mattress from rain, and sheltered the injured cub from the rain. At the resthouse, the forester Bishan and I washed the wound with a mix of turpentine oil and antiseptic lotions, while the cub stared helplessly at us. It couldn't sit and refused to take the pieces of chicken we offered and didn't hold out despite our best efforts.

The mortality rate in a litter is high and it is accepted that only one or two reach maturity. Here was a graphic example about a one year old's inability to fend for itself. Cubs normally need the mother's attention for two years before they can hunt on their own and are strong enough to defend themselves from other tigers. A cub's first lessons in hunting begin with its attempts to catch mother's flicking tail. Unlike lions, the tiger leads a solitary life and a mature pair will be together only to mate, for the one week of oestrus. Mating takes place many times during the day, because for ovulation the tigress needs to copulate frequently. After mating, the male and the female go their separate ways and the pregnant tigress fends for herself. The gestation period is rather short, of 105 days, and the tigress is inconvenienced but not disabled by her pregnancy in hunting for food. Newly born cubs are small and helpless, but the tigress is a fond and caring mother and normally does not let them stir out of the lair till they are about 3 months old. A tigress frequently changes her lair to avoid the attention of other predators and male tigers; the latter are prone to attack male cubs and sub-adults. As sub-adults they will no longer be tolerated by the dominant male in the territory. The male tiger will fight savagely with potential rivals and cases have been recorded of a tiger killing and eating another.

One day at Kanha we came across a tiger which had killed a sambur. It is India's largest deer, weighing about 300 kg. The kill was half eaten and lay in a shallow, open nullah. The tiger was busy chasing away the crows and vultures, roaring at them from time to time. Hearing the roars the riding elephants

became nervous. The mahouts felt that the elephants might stampede and topple me from the tripod when the tiger charged next. Taking a risk we separated the tall tripod from the riding elephant and I was on my own, with the elephants about Seven metres behind me, their mahouts forcing them to stay their ground. I wanted to get the full charge of the tiger's attack on film and a good opportunity came when he chased the birds in my direction, frightening them with an ear-splitting roar as they fluttered into the air. But he ignored my presence. And when I looked back I found that the elephants had run back 18 metres. If the angry tiger had turned in my direction and merely pushed at the tripod, I would have been flat on the ground ready to be mauled and put away for ever. Rajesh knew how vulnerable I was. He forced the mahouts to move in quickly and rescue me, but the elephants were shivering in fear and would not budge forward for quite some time in spite of the coaxing and shouting of the mahouts.

When we learnt that a tigress with three cubs, about ten weeks old, had been seen at the Mukhi range in a different part of the Kanha National Park, we located her quite easily and began to spend whole days with her. She turned out to be friendly and didn't mind the intrusion, at a respectable distance, of the riding elephants. For a week we were able to film the cubs playing and suckling. Then she disappeared for ten days, apparently because a pack of wild dogs had moved into the area. Wild dogs are rapacious predators and a tigress with cubs will immediately vanish on their arrival. Ten days later a mahout spotted a pug mark. We located the cubs above a nullah, but there was still no sign of their mother; she may have been on a hunt. The next day we left the rest house early so that we could cover the two-hour elephant ride by dawn. As we neared the nullah we noticed the tigress sitting in a majestic posture on a nearby mound. The carcass of a half-eaten leopard lay beside her, which the tigress was clearly guarding. It was a most unexpected sight. Barely had we moved closer to her that she took the kill a hundred metres away and started feeding on it, while we filmed her. She held the body between her paws, peeled off the leopard's skin with her rasping tongue and bit into the flesh. Her grand display lasted for nearly thirty minutes, possibly more, before she moved away, to drink water. It gave us an opportunity to survey the area, which did not have much undergrowth because of a summer forest fire. It seemed that the leopard had come early in the morning while the tigress was with her cubs. There were deep claw marks on a tree, suggesting that the leopard had attempted to climb it to escape the tigress' wrath, when it was dragged down. It was the first instance of its kind that either of us had come across.

Tiger country has shrunk enormously in India, because of the calamitous deforestation that has taken place in the twentieth century. There are hardly any forests to be seen there any more and the area is devoid of wildlife. Therefore, the steering committee of Project Tiger, headed by the then Prime Minister Indira Gandhi, rightly decided in 1982 to enlarge six tiger reserves and create four additional sanctuaries. The project has been eminently successful, but some parks have become saturated and there are no buffer zones to accommodate the spillover of tigers. In our family, father and the two of us are convinced that it is scientifically proven that a tiger reserve is saturated with the big cats, culling has to be resorted to the interests of conservation, as is the practice in other countries. By organising selective tiger shoots the government can also earn foreign exchange from rich hunters.

At the Corbett and the Dudhawa reserves, incidents of man-eating have tainted the efforts of conservationists and there is increasing conflict between the tiger and the villagers living on the outskirts of the reserves. One of the tragic deaths that took place at the Corbett Park recently was that of the British ornithologist David Hunt, who used to bring groups of bird-watchers every year from England. In 1985 he was trailing an owl when he was attacked. The tiger sat over Hunt's corpse and was reluctant to leave his kill even though forest guards fired in the air. Hunt was killed very close to the spot where we used to picnic in the seventies. Many of the areas we used to trek in, then, are places where forest guards fear to go these days and will not allow tourists to trek, because these tigers no longer fear man. At many of the reserves, tiger-shows for visitors have altered the natural nocturnal habits of the big cats and made them lose the fear of man. At the Ranthambore National Park I was shocked to see a tiger surrounded by six open jeeps, within a radius of nine metres, as if it was an everyday exercise for the big cat. What kind of wildlife tourism would this be, where the animal is not given the respect it deserves? Because of this induced familiarization, these tigers behave as if they were in a circus or in a zoo.

The Striped Killer

The most difficult animal to hunt down is a maneater, because it knows human behaviour and its cunningness enables it to kill human beings. Unless it is captured or eliminated early, a man-eater can wreak severe damage. The illustrious Jim Corbett once brought down a maneating tiger which had reputedly killed 434 people. Not unexpectedly, legends of notoriety and terror are quickly woven around maneaters. In India, divine powers are easily attributed to a wily maneater, because it is believed that the tiger is the chosen favourite of the great goddess Durga.

It was Jim Corbett who first suggested that a maneater is "a tiger that has been compelled through stress of circumstances beyond its control to adopt diet alien to it". In Corbett's view a tiger would turn into a maneater when it became incapacitated – due to old age, injury, the loss of canines or some other reason – and was unable to hunt its normal prey. This view is now widely accepted by biologists. Unable to chase swiftfooted herbivores in the forest, an incapacitated tiger will find cattle easier to kill in villages within or on the periphery of the forest. Cattle-lifting by a tiger brings it in confrontation with man, quickly teaching the animal that it is rather easy to kill the homo sapien. In recent times even some healthy tigers have turned into maneaters. Many believe that the tiger has now lost all fear of man and has included him in his menu.

Several cases of maneating tigers have been reported near the reserves in north India in recent years. Conservationists at the game reserves have sometimes shown a reluctance to act quickly against maneaters, compelling the villagers to poison them. Many tigers have been poisoned by hostile villagers, who ask the unanswerable: Why does the reserve's tiger come into our fields and why does it kill our cattle? It is important that the villagers near conservation projects be provided with wood and gobar gas or fuel, and fodder for their cattle, to stop them from trespassing into the reserves for their requirements. The elimination of a maneating tiger by reserve officials always begets the immediate gratitude of the villagers and this ought to be directed to help the conservationist's cause.

We had long wanted to make a film on maneaters and the opportunity to begin it greeted us at the railway station of Jabalpur, Madhya Pradesh, enroute to the Kanha National Park. At the railway station we met the park's director, A.S. Parihar, who said he was going to shoot a maneater. He had spent more than a month tracking the maneater and hoped to eliminate it in the coming week. We changed our plans on the spur of the moment and accompanied him to the camp they had set up, near a spot where a tigress had killed one and attacked two others in three separate incidents. She had been declared a maneater by the State government but efforts to trap her had been unsuccessful. There was no alternative to hunting her down. Shortly after we reached the camp, the tigress came up to the tents one night and stood watching the elephants. A forest officer fired at her, but his aim went awry. This added to the local myth about her divine powers. She disappeared from sight for a few days and did not touch the several baits that the forest rangers had posted. It was when three elephants were used to track her down in the forest that the park director spotted her again, as she moved at the elephant's approach. But his shot from the moving elephant went between her legs. She had outwitted them for the second consecutive occasion. As pressure from the local people and the media increased, round-the-clock patrols were set up. Plaster casts of all pug marks seen in the area were made, so that the maneater could be identified and tracked down. The forest officials also set up a well camouflaged trap along the path regularly used by the tigress. A buffalo calf was tethered, in full view, in the middle of a small enclosure which had only one way into it. The trap was tested to make sure it worked. If a man's weight could spring it, then so would the tigress'. However, the tigress ignored the trap. Pug marks clearly showed that she had stopped by the entrance and moved on. Maneaters are not easily deceived. The local people were terrified and restless and called upon a tribal priest to perform rites for the death of the tigress. Then, next morning, reports came that the tigress had made a kill and crows indicated the spot where the half-eaten carcass of a buffalo lay. This was the chance. The tigress would probably return to finish its meal. Very quickly a small area around the carcass was cleared to provide better sighting.

Nearby was an old hunting machan, about nine metres high and the director decided to wait there for her. I accompanied him on his vigil. At sunset we heard a tiger alarm, as a peacock called behind us. I turned to take a look and saw a big tigress approaching from our rear. She paused for a while near the machan before moving to the kill. The director took aim with his rifle, I carefully placed an eye on the cameras and within two seconds of his shot I had the camera in motion. He got her on the shoulder, the bullet going through her heart, but he pumped another three or four bullets into her before he was satisfied that she was dead; for a wounded tiger could be far more dangerous than a healthy animal. Even though the animal appeared to be lifeless, A.S. Parihar felt it was better to make sure. So we carefully aimed a few stones at her to convince ourselves that it was safe to leave the machan. On examination, she turned out to be a perfectly healthy, seven-year old tigress, quite capable of catching wild prey. There was no loss of canine teeth. The paws showed no sign of damage or wounds nor the retractable claws. But she had been a killer. She was one metre high and her length, from nose to tail, was 2.65 metres.

We also discovered that the tigress had milk in her teats. One of the mahouts milked a small bowlful from her, mixed it with wheat dough and took it as a tonic, in the belief that he would imbibe some of the tiger's power. The dead tigress was the mother of two infant cubs. She, perhaps, attacked villagers in retaliation when they ventured into the jungle close to her cubs. Significantly, she did not eat any of her three victims. Paradoxically, the tribals, also worship the tiger. The local people asked that the tigress should be taken to the village, so that everybody could see the killer. Thousands of people came to see and touch the dead tigress, bowing to her in reverence. So big was the throng of people who came that a guard had to be posted to prevent people from taking bits of the fur or even the whiskers. Several people came up to A.S. Parihar and said that while it was good that he had killed this tigress, he shouldn't kill any more, "even if it eats us."

It is said that the tigers of the Sunderban forests in West Bengal are habitual maneaters who prey on local villagers, pouncing from behind to seize the victim's neck between their massive canines. The Sunderbans are the largest mangrove forests in the world. A third of the forest lies in Bangladesh. On the Indian side there is a population of over 300 tigers, distinguished by the title of the Royal Bengal tiger. These mangroves are inundated by salt-water creeks and estuaries and the tiger population is dispersed over countless islands. With an estimated 500-600 tigers, it has the largest single population in the world.

In 1986 Rajesh made his first trip to the Sunderbans and discovered that 'widow villages' dot the mangroves. Maneating tigers have been an age-old problem for the people living there. They produce only one crop of paddy in twelve months and supplement their income by collecting honey and firewood in the forest and through fishing. Despite the perennial threat from the tiger, the villagers say they have no option but to accept the risk or else they will die of hunger.

"Such is the dread of the tiger in the mangroves", says Rajesh, "that gunmen accompany boats on the waterways and

the boatmen will not let you get down without two armed escorts, one in front and one in the rear. You constantly feel that a tiger is lurking in the foliage close by. They say that the Sunderban tiger is so cunning and mean that he knows how to snatch people in the oddest circumstances. The tiger here is notorious for not leaving a kill even if confronted by a group or pelted with stones." English officials, posted in the Sunderbans during the colonial era, have written alarming accounts of their encounters with the maneaters. In the waterways at night the boats are always anchored in mid-stream, though instances are known of people being lifted, while asleep, from anchored boats. The Sunderban tiger is an extremely good swimmer and Rajesh was given a detailed account about one who swam about 10 km to find a mate in Bangladesh.

The Tiger Project agency at the Sunderbans has erected watch towers at two islands for tourists and wildlife scientists. A barbed wire enclosure starting from the pier provides a protected entrance to the watch tower. On his third trip to the Sunderbans, Rajesh began with a night watch at the tower on Nitidhopani and heard tiger mating calls on the very first day, just as the sun began to set. Around 1 a.m. at night he saw a big male moving towards the fresh-water pond in front of the tower and drinking from it. There was a high moon and visibility was reasonably good. A little later he saw the female moving towards the male, but then they disappeared in the direction of the pier.

Rajesh's luck turned the next day. Around noon he saw the male tiger return to the waterhole and he immediately began filming. In its wake followed the female, coming through the Hital forest on the right. They mated twice by the waterhole, as the camera whirred sweet music in Rajesh's ears. It was the first time anybody had studied or recorded the mating activity of Sunderban tigers. In the evening the male pulled out another surprise for the cameraman. Rajesh had spotted a 3-foot long fish lying under a tree very close to a creek. In the moonlight the male could be seen munching through the fish. The forest guards refused to believe him the next morning, but the evidence was undeniable. Fresh pugmarks dotted the spot and all that remained of the fish were its scales. Sunderban tigers are aquatic, catching fish, crabs and turtles in the shallows when the tide ebbs.

Even the barbed wire fencing may not always contain one's fear. One evening, no sooner had Rajesh's boatman entered the enclosure than a tiger roared and leapt at him, squashing the fencing completely. One is always risking one's life in photographing maneaters.

Primordial Beasts

One of the most gruesome and inhuman methods of killing an animal is being practised by rhino poachers in Assam. They killed a minimum of seven rhinoceroses in 1990 alone, electrocuting these magnificent beasts in the remote grassland habitat. Cable leads are drawn by the poachers from high-tension, 11000 volt power lines running overhead and the cables are camouflaged in the undergrowth across rhino tracks.

Unable to see the live wires, the animals stumble into them and are electrocuted. Since rhinos frequent regular spots for certain activities, such as wallowing, scratching and depositing their dung, they are extremely susceptible to these ghastly traps. While Assam's game wardens are severely handicapped by the limited resources and the staff they command to protect this endangered species, world market prices for rhino horn have been continuously rising. Recent market reports say that the price for it in some countries, such as Taiwan, is as high as one million Indian rupees approximately U.S. $ 50,000 per kilogram. It is a matter of concern that the population of the Asian rhino (*Rhinoceros unicornis*), now confined to three areas in India and in Nepal, is rapidly shrinking. In India the only habitat for the great Indian one-horned rhinoceros are the rain-soaked forests of Assam. At the Kaziranga National Park and seven other reserves in the state, the occurrence of about 1300 rhinos is estimated, apart from the very small numbers occurring in the neighbouring area of north Bengal. It was once found all over India.

For wildlifers, the rhino is one of the great attractions of Assam, in itself an extremely picturesque state, famous for its flora and fauna. Along with the rhino, it is also the home of India's only ape, the hoolock gibbon. Other rare animals to be seen exclusively in Assam are the clouded leopard, the golden cat, the pygmy hog, the hispid hare and the golden langur.

The adult one-horned Indian rhino weighs around 2000 kg. The horn which protrudes above the rhino's mouth is composed of a concentrated mass of horny fibres. Despite its fearsome appearance, the rhino does not use the horn as a weapon. Instead, it attacks with its peculiar tusks which are actually large, protruding teeth. Few animals dare challenge the rhino in the forest. It is a quiet animal known to display its temper only when disturbed.

Forest guards in Assam forbid people from tracking the rhino on foot. In the tall elephant grass there is a constant danger that one might run into one-horned giant, which will not tolerate a human intruding into its domain. The rhino charges without any hesitation and can inflict lethal injury. It was with great difficulty, therefore, that Rajesh somehow managed to persuade the rangers to permit him to go on foot to a distant lake known to be a special favourite of the animals in the area. From the back of a riding elephant Rajesh had earlier spotted as many as nineteen rhinos wallowing in the water. But had he taken riding elephant closer, they would certainly have withdrawn. Rajesh felt that he could get exceptional photographs of the rhino's behaviour in water only if he took the risk. He was accompanied by an armed guard and a local helper. The guard was familiar with the terrain and led them along rhino trails. Rhinos follow regular routes. Trampling the undergrowth with their colossal weight they soon chart out a network of 'tunnels' through the tall jungle grass. These trails are easy to follow, but there is the perpetual danger of running into an armoured giant as one walks along. They were making their way cautiously when Rajesh thought he had picked up the sound of a rhino coming towards them. Neither the guard

nor the helper were sharp of hearing. They dismissed Rajesh's warnings and walked on. Barely had they made their way a bit further when they ran smack into a huge creature. It stood but six metres away and immediately launched a full blooded charge at them. It seemed to be curtains for the trio. The animal was too much close. But with tremendous presence of mind the forest guard immediately fired into the ground to stop the beast. The rifle's loud retort managed to frighten it off, saving them in the very nick of time.

Flush with the excitement of their escape they continued on their way and the adventure had its great dividends: Rajesh got some exceptional pictures of rhinos rolling in water and of a female sleeping with her calf. The rhinos love cooling their huge bodies in water. Sometimes they will be seen feeding in small scattered groups of less than a dozen, but essentially the rhino is a solitary animal, satisfied with a limited territorial preserve (0.75 to 5 sq. km). Rhino meetings are marked by ritualized displays, such as the curling of lips and the baring of tushes. They will snarl and grunt aggressively, but serious battles take place during the mating season only. Mating is also tinged by an aggressive display, as the male noisily chases the female before she permits him to mount her. A single calf is generally delivered, though occasionally a mother has been known to deliver two. The calf is pink-coloured and will stay in its mother's protection till it is 3 or 4 years old, because till then it is vulnerable to the tiger. Rhinos normally live up to 50 years.

Traditionally, rhino horn is believed to represent the *linga*, the male organ. Horn powder is used for making aphrodisiacs and even sadhus wear talismans made from its hide and horn. Cups carved out of rhino horn are believed to have magical qualities. Many other parts of the Indian rhino are used as a cure against diseases and are believed to bring good luck.

The rhino reserves of Assam are also home to the wild buffalo (*Bubalus bubalis*). A strong, aggressive animal with long curving horns, it is also distributed in small areas of Orissa and Madhya Pradesh; and in Nepal. It is the most dangerous and fearless of Indian Bovidae and will make a sudden and unprovoked attack. During the mating season the weaker bulls are driven out by the dominant male and these will often mate with domestic buffaloes. Unlike the *gaur* (Indian bison) buffaloes do not shun the presence of man. This can be a danger to the wild gene in the long run.

Ruthless Hunters

The most rarely seen animal of the Indian jungle of central India is the *dhole*, the Indian wild dog (*Cuon alpinus dubhunesis*). It is also the most feared and is notorious as a ruthless killer. It is so difficult to spot that at the turn of century the British settlers thought that the dhole was a mythical animal. Villagers in the forest-areas of Madhya Pradesh, and in Tamil Nadu and Kerala in the south, will often talk of it, but very few photographs of the dhole are to be seen; and few of its activities had been recorded. Though they hunt in packs, the dholes are creatures of the dark depths of the jungle and we are proud that our film *The Whistling Hunters*

is the first visual record of dhole behaviour and its life in the jungle. The dhole is an amazing dog which does not bark or howl like wolves. Instead, it whistles. It is like the sound made when whistling into empty medium-bore cartridge. The dholes use it to co-ordinate with the other members of the pack, specially when they are on the hunt, and cannot see each other in the undergrowth and a dog or two may lose track of the pack during the chase.

The dholes are ferocious killers though they look like cute red-brown dogs. Such is their reputation as ruthless hunters that at the Kanha we were amazed to see that the tigress we were filming suddenly disappeared with her cubs, because a pack of dholes had moved into the area. It took weeks before we were able to track her down again at some distance. In a mind-boggling incident at the Mudumalai Games Sanctuary, wild dogs bit chunks of flesh from a spotted deer even as a huge python had wrapped his coils around it. The mighty tusker, too, will curl its trunk and bang it on the ground nervously, if it smells dholes. Herds with infants will chase it away as soon as they spot a dog. Dholes spend the day in the cool of the forest. Each pack has a leader, the dominant male, and they come to him to ask for the hunt to begin. As a pack, they have a mood-synchronising ceremony in which they nuzzle and rub their bodies against each other before going to hunt. When hunting in open country they set off at a slow lope in single file to present the lowest possible profile. Their other basic manoeuvre will position some members of the pack on the periphery of the scrub, so that these can intercept fleeing prey. The dholes are voracious eaters and a pack of fifteen can polish off a sambur stag. They eat quickly because, like other animal packs, while feeding they are competing with each other.

We had been on the pack's trail for two months in the Periyar Tiger Reserve in Kerala. We tried to follow them in the forest, which posed many problems. The dogs can only be followed on foot, so there is always the danger of disturbing their prey, or running into a tiger or wild elephants. The dholes are good swimmers and faced no problem in crossing the many nullahs and rivulets in the area, while these were major obstacles for us. The sanctuary is named after the Periyar river, which flows through the Western Ghats, and there are many small islets in the large lake in the middle of the park. We chased them on foot and by boat for months on end. One day, trailing behind a pack from early morning, we were hopeful that we would see them hunt in the evening, when a sambur stag suddenly appeared before them. Paralysed by fear, the sambur arched itself defensively, its stomach sucked in, the tail held high out of reach, as the whistling hunters approached. But the dogs were not hungry and let the sambur go. In one specially beautiful sequence we saw a line of dholes swim across a lake, their furry ears bobbing above the water, their snouts floating past like petals in a brook, their sharp eyes looking this way and that, suspicious of the slightest movement in the forest. The dholes do not keep to a permanent den. After a long search we were finally able to locate a den in the interior of the forest. It was on the bank of a dry

nullah and had several openings, which suggested that it had been deserted by a porcupine or by hyena.

We were surprised to learn that in a pack only the dominant male and the dominant female will mate, while the other members of the pack abstain from sex. Dholes mate from October to November. If there is a dispute over the status of the pack's leader, the defeated male will often retreat to form another pack, leaving to his rival the privilege of breeding for the coming year. Only when the dominant female is pregnant do they start to look for a suitable place in which she can give birth. It must be high enough to offer them a clear view, yet secluded enough to be secure from predators. Hoping to film the activity at the den we placed our camouflage hide at an appropriate place. We had to be extremely careful, because dholes are known to move their pups in their mouths and move to a new area at the slightest disturbance. To camouflage our smell we worked with fresh elephant dung. We spread it over our footprints, encircled the hide with it and Rajesh used some to cover the microphone he had hidden in the bushes nearby. We left the hide there for a few days, so that the wild dogs would become used to its presence.

The dominant female stays with the pups in the den for the first two months, when they are completely dependent on her. She relies on the rest of the pack for her own food. We saw the mother free herself from the suckling puppies and actively nuzzle the dominant male, when the pack returned in the evening. He responded to her entreaty by reurgitating some food, on which she fed. While a domestic dog normally has eight teats, dholes have up to fourteen, enabling the mother to cope with large litters of nine or more. When the pups are out of the den, the adult dogs are extra wary. Despite all the pre-cautions, even a slight shift of our camera lens made them nervous and they sounded the alarmcall. Immediately all the pups rushed back to the safety of the den. The pack never stays away for long, when they have a young family to protect. One of the dogs will stay behind to guard the den when the others go in search of food.

The Tibetan wild dog, the *farra* (*Cuon alpinus*) is no less elusive and difficult to photograph than the dhole. In Ladakh they occur in the open mountain ranges, but only in a very few valleys. Their pattern of movement is not known and it is unclear whether they move down to the lower heights during the severe winter months. Not many photographic records of the farra in either Ladakh or Tibet are available. The farra's existence in Ladakh was unknown even to the forest officials, who were amazed to hear of the heights at which we saw them. Nobody had studied the behaviour of this Tibetan wild dog previously. They are an endangered species and their existing number is not known. Not many Ladakhis have seen them either. We are, therefore, proud to have taken the first detailed photographic record of the farra.

Often confused with the wolf, the farra is a handsome cream-coloured dog with a thick coat of furry hair which protects it from the extreme cold. A mane-like ring of hair distinguishes the male and both the male and the female have thick bushy tails.

We were on a look out for the farra while working on our Ladakh project. We made several inquiries from the locals wherever we travelled. One day our trackers came back with the good news that they had located a farra den at a two-hour climb from our camp. This was actually close to a den which nearby villagers had burnt a year ago. The den we had located was at the point where two high ridges met, overlooking the rapid waters of the Indus. We crossed the freezing, gushing waters of the mountain stream and set up camp at the bottom of the ridge. From there we had to cross a dry gorge and climb up the steep, perilous gradient. The farra den was hidden under a rock just below the top of the ridge. They only had to climb out of their shelter to get a clear view of the entire area. They are extremely alert and possess very sharp eyesight and will notice even the minutest movement made by man, from a considerable distance. Making that arduous climb we were, therefore, constantly nervous that we would be spotted by them. As we approached the area of the den we saw three adult farras climb to the top to observe us. Excited by their presence we pressed on towards the den. Reaching the top we saw the pups' excreta littered around the den, which confirmed that the pups were still inside. That was exciting news! But the only angle from which we could get a proper view of the den was the adjoining ridge, which was a dangerously loose mountainside and as one walked over it the gravel would constantly slide down. We decided to put up our camouflage-hide about 100 feet away, in a wedge between two rocks embedded in the loose slope. We dug out a little cave, just big enough to place a tripod in.

Rajesh took up position within the hide before sunrise the next day. The sun rose within an hour of his arrival and with it came the echo of small stones rolling down the slope, an indication that the dogs were returning. Two of them appeared on the hill facing Rajesh. The male sat far from the den and began staring at the hide, which was quite conspicuous because it is difficult to properly camouflage any kind of a hide on those barren slopes. The female stood behind the male for some time, scanned the area for her own satisfaction and then made her way slowly back to the den. She leapt down from a rock into the den, but perhaps she was concerned by the unex-pected appearance of our hide and came out within a few sec-onds, to sit on a nearby rock, frequently calling out to the pup. The pair stayed around the den the whole day, always wary of the hide. It was only the next day that she brought out a pup and let him suckle her in the open. It was completely black in colour; cute, fat and hairy, like a baby bear. A little later the mother led the pup to a flatter patch and sat and played with it. "All this while", remembers Rajesh, "the male seemed very nervy, constantly looking at my hide and he was very suspi-cious about it." When the female left the pup, it promptly scampered to the safety of the den and she returned to sleep by the male. We filmed one pair attacking a goat in a sequence that establishes clearly that they kill their prey by choking the throat. The remains of a number of farra kills revealed that these wild dogs would eat practically everything,

leaving only the horns and the hooves.

The Birth of a King

Indians have long subscribed to a tradition of snake-worship. Snakes abound in India. It is still not uncommon for this slippery creature to be seen gliding along the wooden beam of a country house or slithering through the thatched roof of a rural hut. One barely steps out of the town limits before one enters snake country. In Kerala, in the deep south, snake-altars can be found in every family compound. In India one grows up with the snake. There are 236 species to be found, only four of these are lethally poisonous. Of these the cobra (*Naja naja*) enjoys a special niche in Hindu mythology. Statues and paintings of Shiva the Destroyer show a cobra wrapped around his neck. And Vishnu the Preserver is popularly depicted reclining on the coils of the hydra-headed *Shesha Naga*. Hindu mythology says that the earth rests on its hood.

Father's interest in snakes far transcended that of his peers. He used to keep a dozen snakes at home, in small cages and jars. There would be cobras, vipers and kraits, and one huge python who would often run away. Father, a local guide, Rajesh and I were once moving on foot in the forest next to Haridvar, when we ran into a python. It was almost twilight, and drizzling, but father immediately decided that he wanted to catch it. He pushed a cleft stick against its neck, and Rajesh and I caught it by the tail. A python can be caught only if you catch it both by the neck and the tail as quickly as possible, otherwise its enormous muscular coils will grab the catcher by the loose end. Once we got a firm grip on it, we had to wrack our brains over what we would carry it back in, deciding that a pair of pyjamas would do. The pyjama legs were tied at the bottom and the python was pushed inside. Just to be sure it didn't break out of the pyjamas, we wrapped the bundle with a loose shirt and brought it back to Delhi.

A cage, with a net on one side, was given to the python as his private home, but its anger knew no bounds. It would hit out as soon as it saw anybody. So we put a thin curtain of cloth over the netting. We pushed a few rats into the cage, but it refused to eat. Pythons can stay without food for months and our snake had gone on a hunger strike. Finally, we realized that we would have to force-feed it. Father took it out and we pushed pieces of boneless meat down its gullet, with the help of a small stick. Suddenly Rajesh and I noticed that father's face had turned red and his eyes were bloodshot. He had held the python's tail under his foot, but during the forcefeeding his foot had been displaced and the python had wrapped itself around him with its lethal coils. A coil tightened around his neck and another ringed his forehead. He was choking and couldn't even grunt for help. As we pulled at it, it refused to loosen its grip around the neck. It took all the strength Rajesh and I could muster to break the python's grip and free our father. We managed to put it back into the cage and heave a sigh of relief. Ironically enough, from that day onwards the python began to eat and Rajesh made constant trips to the New Delhi Municipal Committee office to obtain rats from the Rodent Disposal department.

Having made its point, the python gradually turned more affable becoming so friendly and domesticated in our midst that we began to let it roam about the house. Its friendliness, after it decided to accept our company, was a revelation. It was a mature, three m long python when we had brought it home and the pigments on its skin used to shine and glow. Its presence in our house attracted a horde of visitors, as complete strangers turned up to take a look while it lounged across the sofa or snuggled up an arm. Some of them became our close friends and we still thank our pet python for several introductions. Some others, however, refused to visit us because of their wrong notions about snakes. Life would have carried on happily everafter, but for mother's qualms about having a python around the house just after my daughter was born. Mother had always encouraged father's interest in wildlife and would egg us on as we trotted in his wake, but as a grandmother she had fears she could not overcome. So, one day she gave it away as a gift to a snake-charmer, who was immensely grateful for this beautiful present because pythons are highly priced among them.

At the Kanha National Park, Rajesh chanced upon the amazing scene of a python that had swallowed a one-year-old female spotted deer, something we had never seen before. Sleeping under a *ber* bush, looking like a goblet, its stretched skin looked as thin as a rubber balloon. Butterflies sat upon it, probably sucking at some kind of a secretion. News spread quickly and next morning the python had become a local tourist attration. As luck would have it, its heart had apparently been punctured by a hoof of the deer and it died shortly after. A post-mortem by the park officials revealed a mucous web of eggs along with the body of the spotted deer. The deer was almost completely intact except for the face, which had begun to disintegrate. If a python is not disturbed, it will take about two months to quietly digest its special venison luncheon.

Two species of the Indian python are to be found in the subcontinent: the reticulated python (*python reticulatus*) which is the longest snake in existence and can be over 8 metres long, occurs in Assam, the Nicobar islands and along the border with Bangladesh; and the common Indian python (*python molurus*) which is over 5 metres long. Two races of the Indian python occur and are to be found in dense as well as open forests with rock outcrops. The python has a massive girth and weighs upwards of 80 kg. It is the only snake in the world which sits on its eggs.

In recent years the Indian python's existence has been threatened by the poachers catering to the world's snakeskin industry and it has become yet another species of our wildlife that is being persecuted to dangerous limits.

The king cobra or the hamadryad (*Ophiophagus hannah*) is one of the largest venomous snakes in the world, reaching lengths of 5 m or more and its head is about the size of a man's hand. The longest king cobra recorded measured 5.5 m. It is the only snake to build a nest for its eggs, made of dry leaves and twigs collected by the movement of its body. The eggs are hidden inside a lower chamber, while the mother sits on top of

the mound and guards them. A female may lay as many as thirty eggs and the hatchlings measure 50 to 52 cm at birth. The king cobra is an extremely elusive and secretive animal, specially when the snakes are mating or when the female is caring for its eggs. It has also earned a reputation for its aggressiveness and instances have been recorded of king cobras attacking people along jungle paths.

Rajesh went to the Andaman Islands in the Bay of Bengal in the hope of photographing a king cobra's nest and behaviour, with Romulus Whitaker, former director of the Madras Snake Park. Rom had learnt of a female king cobra incubating her eggs in a nest. He had set up camp in a small hut in the forest. Only two days before Rajesh's arrival, local villagers had killed a king cobra inside the hut and its mud walls were spattered with fresh blood stains. It was an eerie sight and the night became more uncomfortable when Rajesh realized that Whitaker and he would be sleeping on the floor. Guided by a Karen tribal the next day, they went to the place in the forest where a farmer had seen a female king cobra incubating her eggs. King cobras in the Andamans are said to mate in January and build their nest in March-April; the young being born in June. Reaching the site they were surprised to see that the ground around the nest had been tidily cleaned and swept, much as one may expect outside a jungle hut. The female had made a nest out of a pile of dry bamboo leaves inside the thicket. The leaves and the litter that had been swept into a heap and had been pressed down by the weight of the snake. Inside the nest, about 30 centimetres in height and 90 centimetres in diameter, the eggs were incubating in the heat generated by the rotting vegetation.

The mother was not to be seen. The Karen guide was convinced that the female had abandoned the nest, because it had been disturbed. "It was in fear that Rom and I approached the nest to about three metres," recounts Rajesh, "all the stories we had heard about the king cobra's deadly attacks raced through our minds. Rom carried vials of antivenom serum for emergency use and I was spurred on by the fact that no satisfactory photographic records of the king cobra's eggs or its hatching were to be found previously. We scanned the surroundings for a long while, before we were convinced that the female king cobra had deserted the nest." They took a quick look at the eggs and discovered that they had developed cracks and were in the process of hatching. The bite of a newly-born king cobra is poisonous and at one stage Rajesh wondered whether he should photograph the nest from behind a glass shield, then decided to take the risks involved and shoot without a protective cover. On the fourth day of their wait, the first of the sixteen newly hatched king cobras emerged out of the nest's mound. As Rajesh crouched low to reach eye-level to the nest, the baby king immediately raised its hood in an attempt to frighten him. "Though I was a bit scared because I was so close," says Rajesh, "I couldn't help laughing at the threatening posture the little king had assumed." Infant snakes have bright yellow and black stripes and their skins glow in the shaded light of the thicket. The infants quickly climbed up the bamboo to avoid predators like the serpent eagle and wild boar. Rajesh spent hours photographing the new-born kings, in what must be the first such extensive record. Those photographs form a rare component in his vast portfolio of uncommon studies.

The Giants of the Wild

To film or photograph wild elephants in India one must be ready for two eventualities : to trail the herd on foot and to withstand the occasional charge that the jumbo will make. Every year about 150 people are killed in India by wild elephants, mainly when protecting their crops. The rogue elephants are known to chase and kill people, attacking without any provocation. We have had several close shaves ourselves. In an incident at the Corbett National Park we were chased by Lal Kan ('Red Ears'), a brute of a beast, notorious as a killer-elephant, who had trampled several labourers at the park. He had been given his name because the pigmentation of his ears was quite ruddy. With age an elephant can loose his natural pigmentation and the ears and the trunk turn reddish. We were working on our film *Elephant: Lord of the Jungle* and at the Corbett Park we were particularly interested in him. That season, Red Ears was in a state of *musth*. During *musth*, which coincides with the rutting season, a thick blackish fluid is secreted out of the male's temporal gland, located between its ear and the forehead. The male pushes his tusks in soft mounds of clay and strains open the swollen temporal glands. The secretion may occur from a few days to several weeks and the behaviour of the bull undergoes a drastic change. He is in an uncontrollable, unimaginably wild state of mind. A male in *musth* is a ravager, a killer, an absolute terror.

One day we took a quick look at Red Ears about a 100 metres from the road. The forest guard suggested that we take a detour behind him to get a better view as he stood in a clearing. But as we reached parallel to him, to drive across his rear to the other side, he turned and charged. A cloud of dust was swirling around his massive body. We had miscalculated distances completely and were heading for a catastrophic collision. The distance between us was getting shorter every second. It looked as if he would overtake the van at any moment. He could have been running at a speed of 30 kph, which is fairly fast in the fields. We were shrieking at the top of our voice at the driver: 'Faster! Faster!' The forest guard, with a 12-bore gun pointing out of the window, was stunned with fear, though it is debatable whether a shot in the air would have stalled a killer-elephant in *musth*. We barely beat Red Ears to the road, but he would not let up and chased the van for a while. We decided we would never venture close to this killer again.

We photographed elephants in India working entirely on foot. One should be familiar with elephant behaviour to do that. Elephants have poor eyesight, but have a sharp ear and can also pick up smell from a considerable distance. One should always approach them with the wind blowing into you, so that it does not carry one's smell to them. In case one is charged at, it is advisable to run uphill or in a zigzag manner,

which is time consuming for the jumbo.

Millions of years ago there used to be several kinds of elephants, such as the mammoth of prehistoric times. Now, only the African and the Asiatic species survive. They belong to two different genera. The Asian elephant (*Elephas maximus*) popularly known as the Indian elephant, is distributed in South East Asia, through Burma, Thailand, Malaysia, Sri Lanka and India. The largest population of the Asian elephants is in India numbering about 18000, possibly more. Its principal habitats being in the eastern states and in the deep south, a substantial number, around 2000, also occurs in central India and a small number, around 500, in the north. The important external characteristics that distinguish the Asian elephant from the African elephant are: the Asian elephant's ears are smaller; only the male has tusks; it has a more domed forehead; the trunk has only one 'finger' at its tip and the hind foot has four toes. The African elephant is bigger and has larger ears; both the male and the female have tusks; the tip of the trunk has two 'fingers' and the hind foot has only three toes.

Recent studies by natural scientists reveal that there is much about the jumbo's lifecycle and behaviour that was not known in the past. Naturalists have also learnt that elephants have another 'secret' form of communication. As youngsters trekking in the forests we were amazed to discover that scattered members of a herd would often act in a co-ordinated manner when suddenly alarmed. It has now been established that apart from trumpeting, elephants communicate with each other through very low-frequency signals which cannot be heard by humans. These sub-sonic signals emanate from a spot in the elephant's forehead, which has 'tremors' when the sonic station is working. These contact signals can travel over short and long distances and help explain some odd aspects of the jumbo's behaviour. How, for instance, an elephant in heat manages to meet its mate several kilometres away. The elephant is the only mammal yet known to emit these low-frequency signals. Indian folklore features many tales about the elephant's amazing sense of memory.

The largest land mammal, elephants have an enormous appetite, needing about 150 kg of green fodder every day. In fact, even during the night feeding does not stop. They are highly social, living in small family groups where the oldest cow is the leader. Mature tuskers are predominantly loners, but join the female herds for breeding. In summer, when the hot sun begins to shine forcefully, the herd will make for the shade and sleep. The first to settle down for a snooze are the calves. They can sleep for hours provided they are not disturbed. Some will lie down, some sit and rest, while others sleep standing like horses. It is extremely difficult to photograph them while they're sleeping because almost always the herd selects a shady place with luxuriant bushes and trees. Often they are unapproachable. It is only after a few years of experience and several days of tracking that it is possible to get a good picture of an elephant herd sleeping. When an elephant feels hot it will often put the tip of its trunk into its mouth, bring out saliva and spray it over its body. They do not have sweat glands. To keep

their body heat down, they constantly fan their ears. Elephants also throw fine dust over their backs to prevent tick, mosquitoes and flies from penetrating the gaps between the wrinkles where these insects lodge and feed. It was interesting to watch an elephant swishing a leafy twig as a fly swat to ward off flies and insects. Many such pests are smashed when caught unaware by a leafy twig or the tail, ear or trunk. Elephants must visit water once a day. A vast expanse of water is necessary for bathing. Elephants love water and wallow and roll once it takes the weight off their feet. They are expert swimmers and love to play in the deep pools. Sucking up the water with trunk, the elephant squirts it in huge volumes directly into the mouth. It needs as much as 140 litres of water a day.

There are many myths about the elephant's mating. Some believe that they mate in isolation or in the deep water to ease the problem of their enormous weight. We have seen elephants mating on several occasions in the presence of the herd. There is no specific mating season. The gestation period is said to be between 18 to 22 months. We wanted to photograph an elephant-birth as one of the key sequences in our film, but the elephant's bulging stomach makes it difficult to notice when a cow has conceived. Moreover, because of the dense foliage it seems almost impossible to actually film a baby's birth in the wild. We spent three years on it. It proved to be terribly difficult. And when we did succeed, we were smitten by a sense of failure.

We noticed a herd of elephants in a close huddle early one morning. The younger members, on the periphery of the circle, were trumpeting and making aggressive charges at anything they saw – cattle, men and vehicles. An hour or so later the herd moved into the forest. We investigated the area and saw placenta at the centre of the circle where the elephants had stood. Obviously, a baby had been born that morning, but had walked off with the herd.

We followed the herd and saw the mother prodding the new born along with its trunk. The calf wobbled unsteadily, but was helped by the mother and an attendant 'aunt', who used their trunks to help it walk on its own legs. The mother was often resting her head on neighbouring females, because she was herself exhausted by the delivery. The mammary glands are between the mother's front legs and a calf guzzles up to 10 litres of milk a day. But we observed that every member of the herd was very much attached to the new born, as in a human family, and everyone wanted to play with it and was extremely protective towards the calf.

We often wondered whether we would ever succeed. It seemed impossible to film a natural birth. We finally decided to work with camp elephants.

The following year, after a long wait we saw a heavily pregnant female in distress. The labour pains had started. It seemed that the animal we were filming was having her first calf. She lay on the ground for some time, making rocking motions, perhaps to put pressure on the stomach and ease the birth. The sun had disappeared behind the trees. She stood in painful labour. She was taking periodic rests between the pushing and straining. We were excited and hoping that the

birth should take place soon, because the light was fading. Then it looked as if the calf has been moved into position for its entry in the world. She looked in great agony as the contractions became more intense. She started kicking out a back leg to remove any possible obstruction. Bending her rear legs she made the gap between them wider and reduced her height to ease the birth. Then, at last, covered in the foetal membrane, the calf entered the world. As we observed through our viewfinder there was no reassuring movement from the small body. The calf was stillborn. The mother, still not convinced of the inevitable, kicked dust over it in order to dry the calf, because elephants cannot lick new borns dry, as most other animals do. It was all in vain.

An elephant population needs vast stretches of forest for survival. With industrial and commercial development, more forest areas in India are being taken over. Plantations for tea, coffee, pepper and rubber are increasing every year. Traditional migration routes of the elephants have been cut off. Poaching for ivory is the other major threat and the Indian elephant has already been included in the list of endangered species by the International Union for Conservation (IUCN). India has banned all trade in Indian ivory. However, craftsmen are allowed to import African ivory and once it is carved it is difficult to distinguish between Indian and African ivory. Implementing the law has many problems.

Sometimes forest officials discover that they do not have the resources to match the firepower of the poachers, who use sophisticated rifles and walkie-talkie sets during their operations, while in remote areas the guards have only sticks to fight them with. At the Periyar Wildlife Sanctuary in Kerala, you can often hear gun-shots. It has become rare to see an elephant with big tusks and an imbalance in the sex ratio has been created, because the males are being decimated. We have even seen small tuskers killed and poachers have begun to pour acids to pull the tusks out.

It is miserable to see the outrages committed by the poachers. One evening, at the river in the Mudumalai Sanctuary we came across a young tusker, ten or eleven years old, who couldn't drink water because his lower jaw was paralysed. The wound on his forehead was full of maggots. He had been shot at below the jaw and the high calibre bullet had apparently come out of the forehead, opening up a 10 centimetre wide wound from which pus flowed. He was in bad shape, resting his short tusks, which were only a few centimetres long, upon the trunk of a tree. Suddenly we heard an explosion, caused by a labour gang who were blasting the rockside to lay a road, and the tusker's behaviour was immediately transformed. He could associate the blast with his own tragedy. He has looked like the living-dead earlier, but was now full of anger and charged briefly in the direction of the explosion. In recent years poachers have killed over 100 tuskers in south India alone. We informed the forest officials at the sanctuary about the wounded tusker. The next morning all the big camp tuskers were taken to the area to caputre it in a small *kheda* operation. Sitting atop riding elephants, the mahouts tried to put a rope around his neck, but this proved quite difficult, as he would break the rope and run off. The operation lasted for four hours before he was brought under control and finally brought to the camp by keeping him between two big elephants. His wound was treated by the veterinary surgeon, but the effort was in vain.

The Last Refuge

In the mid-seventies Rajesh would spend months on end tramping through the 1155 square kilometres of the Gir forest in Gujarat, the only place in the world where the Asiatic lion (*Panthera leo persica*) is still to be found in the wild. It is now referred to as the Gir Lion. It is smaller than the African lion and the male's mane is scantier. However, it has a denser coat, longer tufts of hair at the end of its tail and on the elbow, a distinctly full fold, and a shaggier fringe of hair on its belly. They also differ somewhat in behaviour from the African counterpart and at the Gir they take advantage of the bushes and stalk prey. The Asiatic lion used to be distributed over West Asia, Iran and the plains of India. However, at the turn of the twentieth century it disappeared from all its traditional habitats except the Gir forest in Saurashtra, Gujarat, which is a rugged country with an undergrowth of thorny scrubs and bushes and open grasslands. The animal has been ruthlessly persecuted by hunters who wanted to boast of their bravery by killing a lion, both in Mughal times and by important VIPs of later ages. It was the Nawab of Junagadh who protected the lions at Gir in forests that were a part of his domain. The lion has enjoyed imperial status in Indian history since early times and the insignia of the great Mauryan emperor, Ashoka, comprised of three standing lions. This is still used by the Indian government as its official seal.

The Gir lion was one of our earliest subjects of study. For Rajesh it had become a second home for several months and, like the foresters of the Gir, he could identify many of the park's lions by the names that the foresters had given them: the brothers Tilia and Ubhada, Lhasa and Bhagat, Sultan and Akbar; and so on. I observed that they rest under the shade of trees and go out in quest of prey early mornings or at dusk. There are also several cases of males living in pairs for many years. Rajesh was unable to photograph the lion's chase and the kill of prey, but this is very difficult to photograph in the thickets of the Gir. On one occasion Rajesh was to be surprised when a lioness mated, in the interiors of the forest, with the brothers Ubhada and Tilia in successive weeks. A strong, aggressive male, Ubhada would not allow anybody to come within 50 metres of him, despite the considerable interaction between the lions and the foresters who patrol the area regularly. Lionesses are normally in oestrus for six to seven days and the frequency of mating is quite high. Rajesh was able to capture the intermittent roars and moans that the male makes during the sexual climax. Between copulation, Ubhada would occasionally charge in their direction, but Rajesh and the forest guards accompanying him would shout noisily, at which he would go back to copulate again. On the fifth day, however,

Rajesh noticed that Ubhada had almost lost interest in the lioness. He had become so weak that he could barely stand. The lioness would rub her body against him seductively, but he seemed to have been drained of all energy. Strangely enough, as if on cue, brother Tilia turned up and began mating with the lioness for the next few days. It was astounding behaviour and none of the guards at the Gir had ever heard of such promiscuity before. Nor did Ubhada protest in any manner whatsoever at the takeover. We have observed tigers copulating thirty-five times a day, with a far greater frequency than the Gir lion, but we have yet to come across a male tiger as exhausted by the exertion as Ubhada was.

The Gir lion population has grown from less than 20 animals early in this century to over 280 by the end of May 1990. The lion and man have shared the forests of Gir for many years and both had shown a tolerance for each other. During the last three years, however, the lions are known to have attacked human beings, claiming over 16 lives and injuring over 140 people. It is possible that the forests are unable to contain the growing number of lions and territorial and social pressures have led to a dispersal of the animals outside the park. The man-lion conflict is heightened by the presence of Maladhari and Siddhi tribal villages within the park and on its periphery. The Maladharis are cattle-breeders and live with their cattle herds inside the forest, instigating conflicts with the lion.

There are several black-maned males at the Gir, but full-grown males do not appear in the vicinity of the various tourist lodges inside the forest. The prides that are shown to tourists by the foresters comprise of lionesses and dependent cubs, who allow the visitors to walk quite close of them.

While tracking a male lion I was advised never to allow the lion to take a position above one's own. Yet, it is possible for the careful naturalist to move on foot in both lion and tiger country. At the Gir forest, Rajesh and I have had many cups of tea in close vicinity of lion prides, sharing the morning view with a small bonfire and in the company of forest guards, we have safely spent many late winter evenings in the forest, confident that we would not be attacked because, having spent so many days in their preserve, we had familiarised them with our presence. However, there have been some moments of spine-tingling adventure. On one moonlit evening at the Gir, Rajesh was accompanied by two forest guards who led a bait, with a lioness trailing five metres behind him. Another morning, while he was clicking away at a pride of lions five metres away, a year old cub ran off with his camera bag. Taught by the forest guards to caw like the crow in an emergency, Rajesh's mimickry prompted the cub to let go of it. It was a bag he treasured for many years, because of the two holes the cub's canines had pierced through its sides.

There is a danger of something going drastically wrong with lion population at Gir and the world could be in danger of losing this majestic beast. In the past, the Government of India has tried and failed to translocate the Gir lion, because of lack of prey and no proper monitoring in the new areas. At the same time, a lot of public money is being unnecessarily wasted by several state governments who have set up local lion safaries by releasing zoo lions in small areas. In most cases, these are African lions, prompting one to suggest that if such safaries have to be established, it might be more rational for the state governments, to stock these with the Indian lion, instead. Such safaries lead nowhere. Instead, a concerted effort should be made to find a second home for the Asiatic lion.

Walking in the Footsteps of the Snow Leopard

A world unto itself, Ladakh, the land of passes (*la*-pass; *dakh*-land) is one of the most unusual and mysterious terrains in the world. An arctic high altitude desert where snowcapped mountains rise above a vista of fine sand, where barren mountain ranges sport unexpected colours in rich ultra-violet light, brackish landlocked lakes stretch for miles on end, narrow fertile valleys sprout barley crops and wild roses against a backdrop of treeless hills, whose flat plateaux shimmer in 37 degree celsius during summer and freeze at night, the mercury dropping to minus 40 in the winter. This is the land beyond the great Himalayan Range, a rainshadow area with minimal rain (92 mm.), comprising three near-parallel ranges running northwest to southeast: the Zanskar, the Ladakh and the Karakoram ranges which emanate from the Pamir Knot and reach up to Tibet. These inhospitable massifs have for centuries been both open and closed to human civilization. Ladakh is part of the forbidden Land. An independent kingdom till it merged with India, Ladakh also represents the last cultural outpost of the old Tibetan order. Yet, it was never part of Tibet politically. In fact, Buddhism reached Ladakh prior to its spread into Tibet and Ladakh was one of the major routes by which Buddhism travelled to Tibet.

Lying at altitudes ranging from 2900 m to 5900 m, between 32-36 N and 76-79 E, Ladakh was closed to the outside world till 1974, when some parts were opened to tourism by the Indian government. In geo-strategic terms, Ladakh is extremely sensitive. It shares a long border with Chinese Tibet and Sinkiang province, with Pakistan-occupied Kashmir and Ladakhi area and its northwestern edge is separated by a thin strip only a little away from western Afghanistan and the Russia. Large parts of Ladakh fall within the inner-line border manned by the Indian army and remain closed.

The great river Indus, originating on Mount Kailasha, flows across the Tibetan plateau into Ladakh Demchok. It runs across the land from southeast to northwest before entering the Pakistan-occupied Kashmir. The Tibetans believe that the river originates from the mouth of a lion and they call it *Senge Chu* ('Lion River'), a name which perhaps, gradually distorted into Sindhu and then to Indus from which the name India was born. Other rivers like the Zanskar, Suru, Dras, Shyok and Nubra originate from the southern and the northern glaciers and join the Indus. Water streams have formed immense landlocked salt-water lakes, of which the Pangong Tso (*tso*-lake). Tso Morari, Tso Kar and Tso Rul are prominent. The largest of these is the Pangong Tso, 150 km long, east to west stretching

beyond the border into Tibet. Since the mountain tops are frozen for the long winter months, Ladakh is even now called *Kha-pa-chan* ('abounding in snow'). The brackish lakes are the remains of a vast network for fresh-water bodies that must have existed in Ladakh thousands of years ago. Ladakh probably had much higher rainfall then. The deep gorges were probably cut by torrential rains.

Ladakhis combine the agricultural and the pastoral life. In the lower vales they cultivate one crop in the year and to supplement their income they maintain flocks of yaks, sheep, goats. The upper reaches are inhabited by nomadic herds people. The Ladakhis have been taking yak and sheep caravans into Tibet since very early times and have traditionally traded with Sinkiang, Central Asia, Tibet, Himachal and the Kashmir valley.

At the top of the food chain in Ladakh is the magnificent, furry, snow leopard, which has seldom been photographed in the wild. Other predators include the Himalayan lynx, the Pallas cat, the wolf, the stone marten and the wild dog. The mountainsides are populated by nyan or the great Tibetan sheep, ibex, blue sheep, urial markhor and wild goats, which are the species preyed upon.

Rajesh and I have been going to Ladakh since 1974, when it was first opened to the outside world. Rajesh soon came out with his book of photographs on Ladakh, with the text written by father. We had always wanted to undertake a comprehensive study of Ladakh's wildlife, though we were uncertain whether the army authorities would allow us to carry our camera equipment to the more inaccessible valleys where most of this exotic wildlife occurs. Fortunately, our credentials were found worthy and we could finally begin work on our ambitious three-year project. The low temperature, the thin high-altitude air and the terrain might be considered highly constricting for outsiders, but Ladakh is a photographer's paradise. You simply have to turn the camera a little to discover a fabulous new picture, because of the dramatic geographical contrasts that the vista presents, as chocolate or zebra-striped or yellow red mountains jutt out of desert-like flats, and fertile green valleys are juxtaposed with the barren but beautifully sculpted hillsides.

The most famous, the most elusive and the most difficult-to-track animal in the inaccessible ranges of Ladakh is the snow leopard. Somewhat smaller than the panther; it has a beautiful, smoke-grey coat with large rosettes and a thick furry tail, almost as long as its body. The Ladakhis call it *Shan* (*Panthera uncia*).

It took a full year, over two winters, for us to finally spot a snow leopard. An animal that has eluded many search parties and naturalists, some of whom were left with no option other than to detail their efforts in pursuit of this elusive and wary Himalayan field. The irony is that scat markings and pug marks of the snow leopard have been seen by many natural scientists and wildlife photographers, who have failed nevertheless to spot the animal itself. So close and yet so far is how one feels while tracking the snow leopard. However, though it lives along the snowline, it is not white as many people presume. It is

known to be shy animal and its grey rosettes on a creamish furry coat helps it to camouflage itself easily in the terrain. Active mainly at night, it is a quiet killer. Unlike the tiger or the lion, whose presence in the forest may be signalled by birds, deer and langurs, the snow leopard's stealthy existence is not generally announced because of the habitat's scarce wildlife. The snow leopard usually inhabits the upper reaches of Ladakh's ranges. It is known to traverse heights upwards of 4000 m in summer, following its natural prey. In winter it descends to lower elevations, but has not been spotted below 3200 m.

Yet, we were determined to study and film this animal which was extremely difficult to track. The task was formidable and we were to have many close misses, embarking on several fruitless trails, being repeatedly outwitted by the elusive, agile leopard of the heights. A summer expedition would have required taking our large team, after due acclimatisation, to very inaccessible ranges. The alternative was to brave the wind chill and the freezing winter of Ladakh, without any heating, when the temperature drops to minus 10 degrees celsius within the tent and can be a numbing minus 40 or more outside. Since the shan is extremely mobile in a rugged territory to which he is well adapted, we realized that it was not possible to go in its trail without an expedition that was well provided for in all respects. We deployed six trackers and several more coolies with our caravan, which included twenty pack-carrying yaks and four ponies apart from a four-member film crew. Moving around the icy slopes and the frozen streams is extremely hazardous. We set up camp at a height of 4877 m where fresh pug marks and scat markings could be seen. It was so cold that the potatoes, the cauliflower, the onions and the other vegetables we had taken from Delhi were quickly frozen. Even the eggs had become as hard as stones. There was no water to be seen. Our cook would go out with a shovel, and bring back blocks of ice, which he would then melt over the fire. As the mercury dipped way below zero inside the tent at night, we would wake up in the morning to see that because of condensation even the sleeping bags were damp with the moisture of our breath.

On dozens of occasions we would come across evidence, which would compel us to set off in immediate pursuit, but the leopard seemed to disappear into the thin mountain air though he might well have been keeping an eye on us. Then, one day, our trackers spotted a domestic goat, killed evidently by a shan about 14 km from our camp, near the Meru village southeast of Leh. The kill had been only partially eaten by the next day, when we set up our hide, but the predator turned out to be rare white lynx. The long erect tufts at the tip of the lynx's ears are black and it has a short stubby tail like the bob cat. It is being persecuted for its valuable fur and its number in the wild is not known.

We continued our search for the snow leopard and our luck turned shortly afterwards when it picked up a goat while we halted near the mountain road. Two of the crew members, sitting in the jeep's backseat, suddenly shouted excitedly: 'Snow leopard! Snow leopard!' Hardly 200 metres away on the other side of the road, an animal ran into the middle of a herd

of goats grazing at the end of the slope. It was 1 p.m., the young boys tending the herd were making butter-tea at a little distance. Only the noisy panic of the goats drew their attention to the predator's assault, but it quickly disappeared among the rocks. I rushed down the slope. The boys said a wolf had attacked their goats. But when I examined the pug marks in the snow it was obvious that this was no wolf. Those, clearly, were the pug marks of a snow leopard. It had killed a small goat, biting at the neck. Stones from the slingshots of the young shepherds and the commotion they had created had frightened it off, but I was sure that it would return to see what had happened to its kill. We asked the shepherds to guard the carcass till I set up a hide and was ready. Then I persuaded the boys to take their herd and leave the area. The sound of the goats and the anxious shepherds died away. The sun had moved behind the hill and shadows began to spread over the valley. I waited patiently for two hours, keeping a sharp eye on the rocks facing me. Then it returned. Standing still for a brief while, looking in the direction of his kill and twitching its tail in the air, I was overwhelmed by the sheer excitement of catching a glimpse of it at last. My knees trembled and my head reeled with joy. I could barely contain myself. It was a young animal, evidently quite hungry, which is why it had dared to attack the goats in the presence of the shepherds. I could see it walking cautiously downhill to the half-frozen stream where the carcass lay. However, though I was only a hundred metres away, it was extremely difficult to spot the furry shan in the fading light, through the viewfinder, as it crept stealthily through the natural camouflage of rock and snow. Only after the noise of a lorry's engine on a road above me, sent it scampering about five metres up the slope and into a ditch, was I able to frame him within the camera-lens when he returned to the kill. The leopard caught the dead goat by the neck and, dragging it between his legs, began to move up the steep climb. The gradient was exacting even for the leopard. From time to time it would run out of breath and stop to rest, before it managed to take its load to a quieter place behind the rock.

A fortnight later our trackers came across a blue sheep killed by two snow leopards, who were evidently a-courting. Thirty minutes after we had set up the hide, the pair made their appearance. They were quite distinct from each other in size and bearing and walked down to the remains of their kill, which they had quite polished off. They had even cracked open the skull and eaten the brains. But their curiosity had been aroused by a lamageier circling above the skeleton and by the ravens that had begun to peck at its bones. A few Himalayan griffin vultures also arrived and a squabble broke out between them and the ravens. But the shan had not left anything for these scavengers. After the snow leopards had completed their checking out, satisfied that they had not left any meat uneaten, the pair climped up the slope and moved away. It was a loose, gravelly hillside and I saw that they were having some difficulty walking over it. Making their way to the top of the hill, the two disappeared. The griffin quickly fed and began to disperse and the lamageier moved in. It is not known as the 'boneb-

reaker' without reason. It began to cut at the joints and dissemble the skeleton. The smaller bones they simply swallowed as they searched for the marrow inside the bigger bones. Although it is a vulture, the lamageier is a beautiful bird, with a creamish underbelly and brown feathers. It has tufts of hair sloping down the beak, which is why it is also known as the bearded vulture of the heights.

It was Rajesh who had our third sighting of the snow leopard within 60 days. He undertook an 18-hour walk over steep terrain to reach the valley where the leopard had killed a young yak calf. A little afternoon, Rajesh arrived at the frozen stream at the bottom of a narrow valley where the yak's carcass lay. He had to carve out a hole in the snow to tuck the hide into the steep mountain slope. Around 3.30 p.m. he saw stones rolling down, but it turned out to be the herd of yaks whose calf the snow leopard had killed. They went up to the dead calf and the calf's mother called to it and licked it plaintively. The other yaks kept sniffing the ground and moved around anxiously. Ladakhi shepherds will have their yak herds to gaze unattended, though from time to time one of the herdsmen will go to check on the herd. Yaks are quite capable of defending themselves in the wild and when they see a predator like the snow leopard they will, like the wild buffalo, form a defensive circle and use their sharp horns to ward off the attack, while the young are protected. There were several young calves in this herd and the leopard had managed to strike a fatal blow at one of them, who might have strayed away.

Rajesh was about to give up hope when he suddenly saw the leopard standing barely two metres away, its long tail twitching in the air, as it stared intently at its kill, ignoring the hide completely. After a pause it went down, picked up the calf and began to drag it up the slope on which Rajesh had made his little niche. "I could never imagine that a snow leopard would come and stand so close to me. I kept absoutely still, giving him no chance to suspect anything. I did not dare take a picture, of course, click of the camera would have disturbed the beautiful animal. Then he resumed his course on the gradient," recalls Rajesh. The leopard was kept slipping on the icy surface and despite its efforts it was difficult for it to drag its kill up the steep slope. It struggled for a while and, becoming exhausted, settled down to eat. The exposure metre in the viewfinder showed that the film was under-exposed, but Rajesh kept the magazine running till it turned completely dark. Around 7 p.m. a full moon appeared and in the moonlight he could still watch the snow leopard eating its meal, with the naked eye; but then our trackers arrived to pick Rajesh up and the predator of the high mountain slowly disappeared in the dark.

The geographical range of the snow leopard covers an extensive area across several countries. It is distributed in the mountain ranges of India, Nepal, Bhutan, China, Pakistan, Afghanistan, the Soviet Union and Mongolia. In India it occurs in Ladakh, Himachal Pradesh, Uttar Pradesh, Sikkim and Arunachal Pradesh. Recent estimates say that there are about 250 animals in Ladakh alone, out of an estimated population of 600 in India.

Guns have now made their appearance in Ladakh and a few

huntsmen offered to sell us snow leopard pelts. I was told that the nomads sometimes get a live yak in exchange for a pelt if they manage to smuggle it into Tibet. The pelts fetch high value in the international market and sell for as much as U.S. $ 5,000 each. It is listed as an endangered species and trade in its pelts or any other article is illegal. In Ladakh some areas have been declared as snow leopard reserves by the State government, but the paucity of funds is telling. There is a negligible number of staff, vehicles, wireless sets etc. to oversee and monitor the vast, sprawling reserves. A system to prevent man-leopard conflicts also needs to be evolved.

The shepherds and graziers in the upper reaches wage an unremitting war against the *shanku*, the Himalayan wolf (*Canis lupus*) which preys upon goats, sheep and yaks and is considered a dangerous pest by them. The nomads' existence revolves around the migration of their flocks in search of new pastures. Wolf packs follow them roaming over vast areas. Normally a pack does not have more than three or four members, the wolves will hunt boldly and without fear of the shepherds. They are voracious and are known to kill four to five animals. Though they are Buddhists, the compulsions of survival have fostered a strong hunting tradition among the Ladakhis and regular village meetings are held to organise the wolf hunts. Search parties of three or four go forth during the breeding season into different valleys and along the streams and nullahs. If they find a den, the search party will kill all the pups except one to bring it back to the village as a proof of their brave act. The killers take the cub from house to house to be rewarded with grain and money and offered chang, the beer-like drink made of barley which is extremely popular all over Ladakh and in Tibet. Sometimes a wealthy nomad will give even a sheep or a goat as reward. Considerable sums are also collected by the hunters. Therefore, when we asked to be guided towards a possible wolf den, where we could film the rearing of cubs, our inquiries were mocked at and derided, because in most villages they had already been killed.

During our treks through isolated valleys we often came across primitive stone-traps, made by lifting one end of a large stone atop a sturdy bone, which acted as the bait. Once the wolf pulls at the bone, the support collapses and the wolf's head is crushed under the heavy stone. The more sophisticated trap used by the Ladakhis is the *shangdum pit*. The entire village pools its energies to maintain the deep pits at regular crossings or routes used by the wolves. The round traps are made with stones and at the centre of them is a small raised area on which a goat or a donkey is tied. The villagers bring water and food for the bait until it is killed. In winter the wolves find prey rather difficult to track and are therefore tempted into the trap. A hungry wolf or a family of wolves will jump into the shangdum, tempted by the bait, to soon realise that it is a trap. They are then stoned to death. In their search we came across a hungry loner who was unable to walk. Disturbed by our horses a Tibetan woolly hare (*lupus oiostolus*) came out of the bushes. The wolf started chasing it, then suddenly a golden eagle pounced on the hare, snatching it away in

talons, but it slipped and fell in the rocks below. Our horsemen rushed to pick up the hare and had a feast in the evening. However, not many of Ladakh's Buddhists eat hare and other animals which have incisors and are without horns and antlers. We were camping in winter in Pakse valley, at about 5273 m, to film the wolves that were active in the area. They had killed a yak a few days previously. The villagers activated the shangdum, which proved successful. Within a month they killed two wolves. Villagers will cut off the dead wolf's tail and the head and its skull is used in an elaborate ritual in which the lama prays for peace in the village. Many of these rites hark back to the animistic Himalayan Bon religion, practised by the Ladakhis before the arrival of Buddhism.

While driving through the sandy flats of Chang-thang, we came across the beautiful wild ass *kiang*. During India's war with China in 1962, and because of the military build-up thereafter, there was a catastrophic decline in Ladakh's population of kiang, Tibetan wild ass (*equus heminous*), which is listed as an endangered species. But the kiang population in Indian limits has been steadily rising in recent years. Once relished as a delicacy by the poorest nomads of the Chang-thang plateau, it is no longer killed for meat by Ladakhis. Across the border in Tibet, however, kiang is eaten by the Chinese troops. This has probably prompted kiang herds to migrate from Tibet into India and, in my estimate, there could be about 1500 of them roaming on the eastern plateau. Kiangs generally move in small herds of 10 to 15, but large herds up to 100 or more were common in Tibet. Even in Ladakh herds up to 60 have been observed. We have also occasionally spotted a lone male following his own diktat. The dominant male does not quite tolerate the presence of other males in the herd. It is regarded by some as a distinct species, and by others as a race of the Asiatic or the Indian wild ass found in the Rann of Kutch in west India. In the Rann, the wild ass inhabits the marshes close to the sea, whereas the kiang have adapted themselves to the arctic-desert conditions of Ladakh and have been seen near the snowline at a height of 5791 m. In winter, when not a blade of grass is to be seen across the landscape, the kiang can smell out underground tubers and digs them out with their hooves. The kiang male is the bigger and better-built than its cousin and has thicker coat and a slightly darker colouring. The bigger male will be mistaken as horse from a distance because the kiang has both horse and ass characteristics. On the barren rockface of Ladakh, the kiang easily outruns local horses. Its ability to run at high speed over longer distances enables it to keep predators at bay and even the ferocious wolf packs are rarely able to hunt it down. Occasionally, kiangs will raid village crops. Confrontations between kiang herds and Ladakhi shepherds, who want to preserve the limited pasture-lands for their own flocks, have increased in recent years. The population increase has provoked complaints to government agencies from the nomadic shepherds in eastern Ladakh. They want the kiang to be driven back into Tibet from where they have reportedly migrated. In the marsh by the Hanle river, we saw two separate herds grazing peacefully along with yaks,

sheep and horses. When we ventured too close to one of the herds, they twitched their tails nervously and ran off; stopping from time to time to turn and take a look at us.

Ladakh attracts large flocks of migratory birds during summer. They are drawn by the abundant insect life in the alpine pastures below the snow line. Many of these breed exclusively here. Over 170 species of birds have been identified in Ladakh, but only a handful of these will stay through the harsh winter, such as the lammergeier, the golden eagle, griffon vultures, red and yellow billed choughs, snowcocks, chukors, magpies, Tibetan ravens, grey tits and sparrows.

The bar-headed (*Anser indicus*) is the most beautiful goose in the world, in my opinion. It is the legendary Indian bird, the *rajhans*, subject of many poetic descriptions and is the chosen vehicle of Saraswati, the goddess of learning, though it is often misrepresented as a white swan, perhaps because of its long neck. Two black stripes on the head and the neck give it its mundane name and are in sharp contrast to its almost uniformly brownish grey colouring. It has the longest wings among geese, which help them to fly over the mighty Himalayas. They are known to fly as high as jet airliners and have been observed overhead from a height of 8300 m. They can fly up to 3200 km in one stretch. Bar-headed geese winter in the riverine basins of India, Pakistan and Bangladesh and migrate in summer to breed in high altitude lakes of Ladakh, Tibet and China.

The brackish Tso Morari and the fresh water portion of the Tso Kar are the only known breeding ground in India of these geese. The floating nests of the great crested grebe can also be seen in the shallow waters and in the cliffs rising on either side the brahminy ducks build their own nests. Seven months in the year, the Tso Morari lake in eastern Ladakh is cut off from the rest of the world, accessible only through an arduous journey by foot or on horseback. The Ladakhis have an interesting story behind the naming of the lake. Legend says that a *chomo* (Buddhist nun) riding a yak was carried into the lake. At first the yak swam boldly and the *chomo* was delighted; but after a time the animal grew tired and began to sink in the water. The *chomo* became frightened and screamed out *Ri-ri Ri-ri* in fear, until the yak sank and she was drowned. Since then the Ladakhis have always called the lake *Chomo Ri-ri,* which has been corrupted, in bureaucratese to Tso Morari.

Bar-headed geese begin arriving at the very onset of summer, in May, when a slab of ice two to three feet thick still covers the waters of the lake. The fresh water streams on its northern edge, are partially frozen and a tapestry of snowfields hangs down the mountain slopes. Perhaps the highest village with cultivation in the world is Karzok, a small settlement on the periphery of the lake. As the howling wind cuts through the lake's frozen top and ice blocks crash against each other, the geese begin selecting sites for nesting on the bald patches of a small island. The difficult snow-covered approach to Tso Morari had thwarted previous expeditions by Indian ornithologists and little was known about the nesting and breeding behaviour of the bar-headed geese till Rajesh and I managed

with great difficulty to reach the place, hoping to photograph and film their lifecycle. From the frozen edge of the lake we spotted a flock of geese on an island. We soon named it Bar Island. The early arrivals were guarding their nesting sites. The males displayed aggressive postures, lowering their necks and honking raucously. Sharp, bitter battles for the possession of prime sites could be observed and the males inflicted serious injuries on each other. In the evening we observed the arrival of three Tibetan ravens on the island. Puffing up their feathers and bloating themselves, they tried to scare the geese off. Then, through the long lens, we saw a raven hopping around to steal an egg. The law of the jungle had, sadly enough, taken over yet again as we watched helplessly. It was only a week after our arrival at Karzok that the ice blocks melted and we could take our boat towards the island. The Tso Morari has great variations of depth. At some places the crystal clear water is so deep that it makes one nervous. At other points the lake was so shallow that our boat would get stuck in mounds of mud. A submerged weed forest spreads for miles together and the water is freezing cold even in summer.

Every day more geese arrived on the island. Though a ring of grass circled the edge of the island, the geese preferred to nest on barren ground, close to each other in a colony, to prevent attacks from predators. The male and the female would swim side by side, dipping their necks in the water from time to time in a ritual ceremony. Then the male would mount the female to mate while they swam, holding the female's neck in his beak. As they separated the male would proudly display his wings, rise vertically and appear to majestically walk upon the water in an unusual ceremony to commemorate conjugal bliss. Unlike other geese, the bar-headed female goose digs a nesting hole with her feet and stomps to flatten the base of the nest. She picks out sand meticulously and throws it around the nest with her beak. Once she begins to lay eggs she will line the nest with her down to keep the eggs warm. The geese lay 4-9 eggs depending on the bird's age. The female is a dedicated sitter and will not stir out for hours together, going away only to drink and bathe. The breeding pairs of the geese do not feed during incubation, which lasts nearly a month. The male stands close to the nest in faithful attendance. The geese are dedicated spouses and pair for life.

The bar island was soon crowded by a colony of nests. While the females sat on the eggs, the males would continuously squabble with each other. Occasionaly, eggs would roll out of a shallow nest or get crushed during the fracas. The nesting females did not display the ability to roll the eggs back into the nest. Eggs were scattered among the nesting females, to be eaten by ravens and gulls. As soon as ravens or the brown headed gulls descended to feed on the eggs, the geese closest to it would sound the alarm and try to chase them off, but the ravens were adept to the game and would raid the island several times in the day. They feed on broken eggs and even steal the eggs from the nest in spite of the vociferous resistance of the geese. The ravens hold the large 130 gm. egg in their beaks and fly to an undisturbed spot. Rajesh and I have

also watched the mother goose being tempted to feed on her own broken egg. The geese display greater aggression among themselves during the breeding season. A pair returning to their nest, after a drink at the edge of the island, would be cowered down by an unwelcome fusillade of honks and would dart, head down, to their permitted quarter. Once they were safely home, the male would raise his head and flap his wings in a majestic display of his prerogative.

Rajesh and I had been waiting patiently for 26 days, but there was still no sign of the eggs hatching. We knew that a common hen's egg will hatch in 22 days, but were not sure when the geese had laid their eggs.

Then, early one morning at around 8 a.m., the first three hairy, bright yellow chicks hatched in a nest. All the eggs in a nest will take eight hours to a full day to hatch. The female will spread her wings and cover the chicks to keep them warm and to prevent them from stumbling out of the nest. We observed that newly hatched chicks were finding it difficult to recognise their parents, who were trying desperately to communicate with them by lowering their necks and calling. I saw an adventurous chick who did get away while its mother waited for her other eggs to hatch. The other females on nest attacked and killed it mercilessly. Once all the chicks are hatched, the parents escort them to the lake. Though the chicks swim from day one, initially the mother will pick out mosquitoes, which happen to breed at that time and feed them. As the chicks grow up they begin accompanying their parents on raids into the barley fields of Karzok causing considerable damage. By the time October comes they will be big and strong enough to undertake the flock's long flight to the south.

The bar-headed goose is the second most endangered among geese of the world and its population has been continuously declining, because it is still hunted as a table bird. Some experts say that only 10 to 15 thousand birds survive today.

The breeding season of bar-headed geese coincides, as at Tso Morari, with the breeding of the great crested grebe the same species to be found in both Asia and Europe. The courtship behaviour of this skilful diver is well-known for its graceful displays. The grebe raise their necks and shake their heads and perform a ceremonial dance. The female lays five to six eggs in a floating nest made of weeds collected from the bottom of the lake. Both the male and the female share nest building and will incubate the eggs. When alarmed, they cover their eggs with weeds before swimming off. When the eggs hatch the parents pluck out their own small feathers and feed the chicks. The male spends as much time as the female in looking after the little black and white chicks. After all the eggs have hatched the parents carry the chicks tucked under the wings, to protect them from predation while the parents are swimming in the lake. One male grebe astounded us by catching a small fish in the brackish Tso Morari, with which it fed its chick. It seems there is some life near the fresh water inlets though many people believe that there is no life in the brackish water. If a chick fell into the water they would spread-eagle their feet, providing a kind of pier for the uncertain little

chick, who had not yet mastered its swimming skills.

Rajesh had several demanding moments at the narrow horseshoe island on which he was filming the grebe. There were two nests in the shallow water, but the high tidal waves of Tso Morari would often swamp the low island completely. The hide was being regularly flooded and Rajesh did not know where to sit during his long vigils with the camera. He finally solved the problem by using a small drum as a stool, sitting cross-legged on it, to keep his feet above the freezing water. On one occasion a fierce thunder-storm lashed the island and threatened to wash away the floating nests. Rajesh saw a nest tossed by the waves which pushed it away from the island and it sank in the deep waters. He rushed out, with the heady desperation of the wildlife photographer, to stop the other nest from being washed away, as the parent grebes chased vainly behind it. Rajesh felt it was imperative to avert yet another tragedy for the grebes. He realized that if the second nest was also destroyed by the tidal waves, it would completely undo our long, patient vigil to photograph the hatching of the chicks. So, unmindful of the stormy lake, he rushed into the water, waded across to the nest, held it in his arms and slowly pushed the nest back towards the shallow depths. When Rajesh returned to the hide, the grebes moved to the nest without the slightest hesitation. It was providential, because the eggs started hatching the very next morning. Rajesh was rewarded by the opportunity to film the hatching and the rearing of the chicks.

To the east of Tso Morari lies Hanle Valley, one of the largest marshes in the Chang-thang plateau. It is one of the few valleys in Ladakh where the rare black-necked crane (*Grus nigricollis*) come to breed in summer. It is here that they find the sweet tubers of the sedge which is a favourite with the cranes. The courtship ritual of the black-necks is most spectacular. They trumpet in unison, bowing, spreading their wings, jumping in the air and toss about tufts of grass. One of the most majestic of birds, it has a dark neck with a shiny red patch on its head and a stumpy, bushy black tail. Only six or seven pairs visit Ladakh in April-May. The larger population of black-necked cranes breeds in China.

Hanle has a chequered history. The great king Sengge Namgyal constructed the famous Hanle monastery in 1625. It had been one of the important stops for the trading caravans going into Tibet. In the sprawling marsh of the valley a pair of black-necked cranes will breed and rear the young in close proximity to grazing yaks, sheep, goats and horses. After several visits to Hanle, in 1990 we happened to reach there in time to photograph the hatching of the eggs. Rajesh discovered the nest on a small patch of ground, barely 1.20 m by 1 m, rising a mere 3 m above the water of the marsh. Indeed, there was no nest as such, just two brown eggs lying in the grass on a flat patch. We set up a small hide about 50 metres away and focused on the eggs with a powerful tele-lens. We had arrived in the nick of time. The next day a crack was visible in one of the eggs and bubbles of air began to float out. The hatching had started. Both the male and the female could be seen lifting their long legs very, very carefully around the eggs while changing duties. From time to time they gently turned the eggs with their bills. Towards evening all we could observe was a small hole pecked from the inside. Occasionally the tip of the chick's beak would become visible and it constantly called. The hatching took place some time at night. Next morning we saw a brownish-red chick lying helplessly on the ground, unable to move, incapable of rising its neck. It had taken almost 24 hours for the egg to hatch and it took another full day for the chick to dry out and stand up. Its reddish colouring sparkled in the light as the sun shone from behind. It took full three days for the chick to begin walking about, by which time the second egg also hatched. While the first-hatched waited for the other egg to hatch, it spent a considerable time within the warmth of its mother's plumage, The chicks soon displayed a penchant for swimming in the shallow waters of the marsh.

On the first day that the chicks wandered away from the nest with their parents, the adult cranes dug out insects and worms for them. Suddenly that evening a 200-strong herd of sheep and goats strayed in the direction of the family's feeding area. We nervously wondered what would happen. But as the herd came dangerously close, the male raised its long beak in a warning call. It appeared that they were worried that the goats and sheep would trample the tiny chicks. Pausing briefly at the alarm, the herd again began to slowly move towards the cranes. At this, the two birds spread their huge wings in a protective shield. The flock stood and stared at the cranes for some seconds and changing direction it began moving in a detour. It was an amazing sequence to see, and photograph, as the majestic carnes guided the sheep and goats away from their young. By mid-October, the chicks grow to almost adult size and then migrate to warmer areas with their parents.

The people of Hanle valley have enjoyed a long and intimate relationship with the black-necked cranes who visit them every summer. The cranes recognize the loose Ladakhi dress, gomcha, and allow the graziers to share the marshy pasture without any perceptible fear. Ladakhis consider the black-necked crane to be sacred symbol of happy conjugal life. Those birds figure prominently among the frescoes and thangkas (scroll paintings) in the monastaries. Ladakhis have never hunted cranes or the other birds. Influenced by the precepts of the Buddhist religion, they hold that animals and birds are like their parents and that nobody should kill them or harm them for the sake of personal pleasure. Saving a life is of great value to them. They have a strong regard for the smaller animals and birds. Hanle valley is like a protective sanctuary for these animals.

Can India's Wildlife Survive?

There is a growing concern in India for the conservation of our rich heritage of wildlife and to preserve the environment from irreparable damage. Unfortunately, this awareness has not yet filtered down to the grassroot level. It is not to be noticed in the sections of the official machinery not directly involved in the programme to preserve the ecosystem. As I have said before, conservation projects in India are woefully short of funds. Widespread consciousness about preserving the envi-

ronment has to be brought about, to supplement the efforts of the understaffed forestry and wildlife departments in the various states. Industrial, commercial and demographic pressures have severely intruded into the lives of both forest tribals and wild animals.

The conservation crisis created because of man-animal conflicts reveals a common pattern all over India. Whether it is the snow leopard or the wolf in the remote altitudes of Ladakh, or the tiger populations in the different parts of the country, the Gir lion in the west or the magnificent tuskers in the south, whenever wild animals come in conflict with the people an adequate compensation must be paid for the loss of cattle or crops, and specially when the loss of a human life is involved. In most cases the insufficient amounts that are to be given, under law, are handed out after long bureaucratic delays. This adds to the local hostility against the animals. The effort to protect our wildlife will be successful only when these people become motivated and committed to it. Another administrative hurdle concerns the lack of co-ordination between the various Indian agencies involved in conservation work. As of now India's wildlife conservation projects are government-funded. There is a need to encourage the participation of individual citizens in conservation. We believe that naturalists, wildlife photographers and film-makers have an important role to play in carrying the message of conservation to the common people. Their involvement needs to be encouraged by the government in order to nurture an interest among fellow Indians for wildlife conservation. Unless we act immediately, more numbers of the endangered species could become extinct in the near future; and be relegated to mythical animals which our children can no longer see. As of now, the world is losing one life form every year.

Being lovers of animal life and as wildlife photographers we have loved every day that we have spent in the jungle, living and working in close proximity to the charismatic and handsome creatures of the wild. It is a rigorous and demanding vocation, often draining one's stamina, but the excitement is incomparable and irreplaceable. There is a sense of joy at being one with nature, which is a truly transcendental experience. The more closely one observes the unique world of the wilds, the more convinced one becomes that animals, too, have a right to live on the earth, for it is their inheritance as well, not just man's alone.

Right: *Koodkumbhan*, the elephant with the crossed tusks. This bull had the biggest tusks we have seen in 22 years of wildlife photography. These tusks were about 1.8 metres long, worth over U.S. 8,500 dollers in the ivory market. The bull was wounded when this photograph was taken. He was to die shortly afterwards. An elephant tusks symoblize the male's dominent status, but these have also become the harbingers of death.

Early on a winter morning, a herd of sambur feed in the lake at the tiger reserve
of Ranthambore, in Rajasthan. These pools are inhabited by *mugger* crocodiles.

A pair of common laugurs peering over the meadows at Kanha, as the sun sets.
Langurs are preyed upon by tigers, leopards and wild dogs and are extremely wary when
they are on the ground. Following pages: Two 8-week cubs follow their mother. The cub in front has
back stripes which are exceptionally broad. It also has a
crooked tail, which is an aberration.

The little cubs are 10-days old and have just begun to open their eyes. An year old cub from the tigress's previous litter joins them during suckling. Tigresses normally mate every two to three years. This animal, however, had litters in two consecutive years, which is rare. Following pages: An angry tigress snarling at Rajesh's riding elephant at Dudhawa National Park. She was suspected of being a man-eater.

The first photographic record of a tiger feeding on a leopard.
The tigress killed the male leopard which happened to stray near her cubs.
Deep claw marks on a nearby tree clearly indicate that the tigress
had pulled the leopard down while he was trying to escape.
Her three cubs were about a month old then.

Snow leopard is an elusive predator of high altitudes. The grey
rosettes on its creamish fur give it a perfect camouflage in rocky mountains.
They hunt by surprise wild goats, sheeps, rodents. They are endangered
as they are still hunted by locals for their valuable pelt.

Tall elephant grass makes it extremely difficult to photograph
the tiger hunting on prey. This large tigress killed a cheetal
fawn in front of us. We were unable to fully film the tigress's lethal assault,
because we could not position our riding elephant in time.
She carried away the kill to share it with her cubs.

The *gaur*, or the Indian bison, is essentially an animal of the hills.
They have a typical muscular ridge above the shoulders.
They come out of the deep forests to graze early in the
morning or at dusk. The *gaur* is respected as a
symbol of vigour and brute strength in Indian folklore.

Dholes, the wild dogs found in India's tropical forests.
The pack is extremely protective of its pups. Adult dogs pick up a
pup in a desperate move, when three wild boars ventured too close
to the den. While the pups are being moved,
the rest of the pack keep the boars at bay.

In a *dhole* pack only the dominant male and female breed.
The female feeds her pups outside the den, while a sub-adult,
perhaps from the previous litter, suckles with the new-born pups.

A common Indian python rests under a *ber* bush after he has
swallowed a mature spotted deer. Deer are a favourite with pythons,
who will not need food for 8 to 10 weeks there-after.
After swallowing large prey, the python will stay put
at one place till it is digested.

The natural colouring of the whip snake gives it perfect
camouflage in its surroundings. When the wind blows, it will
hold on to the plants with its tail and sway in rhythm
with the foliage. This may help in deceiving pray.

New-born king cobras slithering out of the nest after hatching. The king cobra is
the only snake to build a nest. The female collects a heap of leaves and twigs, using her
body movements, and the eggs are laid inside. Right: The king cobra is the largest venomous snake
in the world. It feeds mainly on other snakes. A young king holds the natrix it has caught.

An Olive Ridley hatchling emerges out of the eggshell. The world's largest
nesting beaches of the Olive Ridley turtle are along the Gahirmata coast of Orissa.
The eggs were considered a delicacy locally and there used to be regular trade in them. Olive Ridleys
are still sold illegally in the food markets of Calcutta. It is now on the endangered list
and is being protected by captive breeding and rehabilitation projects.

Red Crabs Ocypoda scrambling across a beach in the
Sunderbans tiger reserve, where man-eaters take a heavy annual toll.
As Rajesh took this photograph, two gunmen kept an eye out for tigers.
Crabs are fondly eaten by the Sunderbans tiger,
along with turtle and fish.

A great Indian one-horned rhinoceros wallowing in a pool
at the Kaziranga National Park in Assam. Rhinos love playing in water,
but a picture like this one is possible only if the animal is not
aware of the photographer's presence in the elephant grass nearby.

Mother stands patiently as the little calf suckles. Curiously,
rhino calves have a pinkish colouring. The calf is dependent
on its mother till it is 3 to 4 years old.

The great Indian one-horned rhinoceros is the largest of all existing rhino species. Horns fetch exhorbitant prices in the international market. In the Orient people have many medicinal and shamanistic uses for the different parts of the rhino's body. The horn is most valued of all, used in making medicines and aphrodisiacs.

Dissuaded by a herd of wild buffaloes from entering the pool,
a mother and her calf lie by the water's edge.
Rhinos are constantly twitching their ears to pick up
sounds and also to prevent insects and flies from settling.

Wild buffaloes at Kaziranga. They attack without provocation.
However, are often seen near villages. Lone bulls are known to
mate with domestic buffaloes. Wild buffaloes are restricted
to some pockets of northeast India and Madhya Pradesh.

71

A rhino grazing amidst wild buffaloes. They share grazing pastures
and pools at Kaziranga. Cattle egrets gather to pick up flies and insects. Overleaf:
Small groups of adjutant storks look for frogs and fish in the marshes of Kaziranga. The adjutant
stork has a wedge-shaped bill and a large hanging pouch. They are known
scavengers and can sometimes be seen near settlements.

Unperturbed by our presence, a huge *mugger* makes determined
bid for the carcass of a cheetal stag, which had happened to die near the lake
at the Ranthambore National Park. This fully-grown marsh crocodile
pulled the carcass into the water, where a group of them
soon tore it to shreds.

The hump on top of a male *gharial*'s snout. It is the
only crocodilian to have this appendage. The *gharial* is one of three
crocodilian species found in India.

A *gharial* hatchling protrudes out of its shell.
The mother digs her hatchlings out of the nest when they begin
to call, after breaking the shell with their egg tooth.
Right: The *gharial's* characteristic long,
narrow snout is studded with 108 sharp teeth, especially designed
to catch the fastest of fish. The fish is carefully turned
around to be swallowed head first.

We observed that the male *gharial* is as eager to carry the hatchlings and may
compete with the female. However many hatchlings fall prey to birds, turtles and even large fish.
Overleaf: The elephant's eye is rather small compared to its gargantian proportions.
It is known to have poor eyesight and is colour blind.

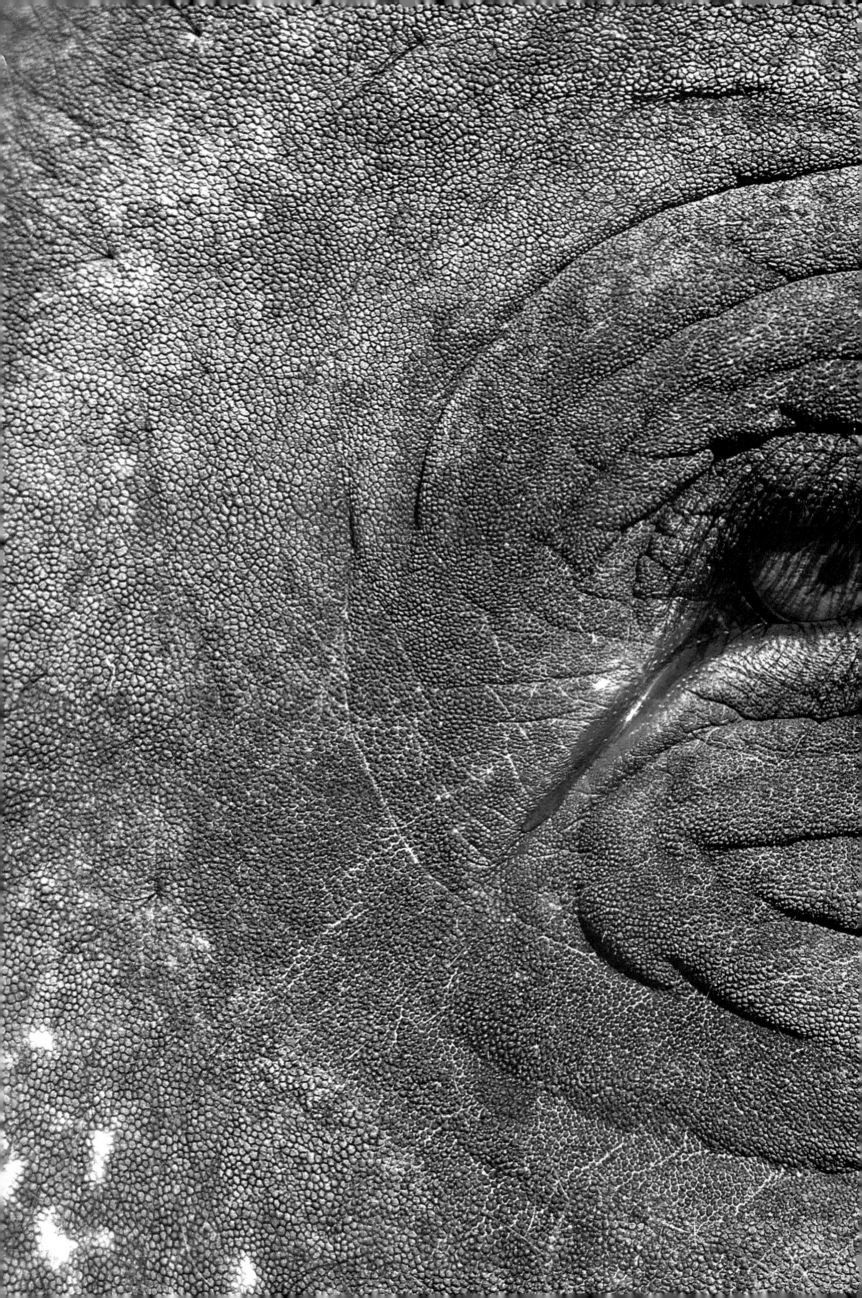

The killer-elephant at Corbett reserve. Red Ears, photographed after we had a narrow escape
when it chased our van. It is in a state of *musth,* when a dark fluid is hormonal secreted from the
bull's temporal glands. During *musth* an elephant is uncontrollably and unpredictably savage.
Right: Many myths prevail about the elephants mating habits, but we found
these to be untrue. It is only the dominant male in the area which will mate
with the cows of a herd. Rivals will be fought and chased away.

Photographing an elephant birth is a near impossible,
nightmarish assignment. After months of waiting we witnessed the birth
of a stillborn calf. It was heart-rending to see the
disbelieving cow-elephant kick dust over her dead calf to dry it,
before she was reconciled to its lifelessness.

Compared to the adult animal, the calf is extremely hairy at birth. It is looked
after by several attendant aunts and at the slightest hint of danger the herd will form
a protective ring around its young calves. It is very difficult to approach a herd
with calves. Overleaf: Elephants move into undisturbed forests to sleep and
not many naturalists have been able to study their sleeping habits. Since an elephant
is mostly on the move, the calves get tired from time to time and need to lie
down and rest their feet. Some of the adults will join the calves and lie down. We
have observed mothers sleeping in the shade close to the young.

In Indian jungles it is difficult to sight the leopard,
because of the dense forests which this feline predator inhabits.
In contrast, the African leopard can be spotted more easily,
specially after it carries its kill up a tree to avoid rival predators.

Small numbers of Siberian cranes migrate in winter from
Russia to the Keoladeo Ghana National Park, formerly known as the
Bharatpur bird sanctuary. Their numbers have declined sharply in
recent years. Fewer cranes are to be seen in each successive year.

The nesting colony of bar-headed geese on an island close to the northern end of
Tso Morari lake. The males will stand in faithful attendance next to the nest. They are dedicated
spouses and pair for life. Preceding pages: A pair of bar-headed geese in Ladakh.

A pair of great crested grebes atop their floating nest.
Both the male and the female incubate the eggs.
Grebes find it difficult to walk on land because of the
positioning of the legs, this may be one reason for
building floating nests in the shallows.

We observed that newly born bar-headed chicks have some
problem in identifying their parents. The parents will, therefore, make
desperate efforts to communicate with them, lowering their necks and calling
out. Chicks that stray away from the nest or from their parents are
often killed by other nesting females.

An aggressive Tibetan raven landing at Bar Island.
We saw a pair of ravens polish off a clutch of 6 eggs in a nest,
despite loud resistance from the goose. The persistence of
the ravens drove the goose to tragic resignation.

The majestic blacknecked crane. Only five or six pairs of this beautiful and endangered
bird migrate in the summer from wintering grounds in Central Asia to breed in Ladakh. Both parents
share the responsibilities of incubation. The first-born will often hide in its
mother's plumage as they await the hatching of the other egg.

A pair of blacknecked cranes are alarmed to see a flock of goats and sheep stray near their chicks in Hanle valley. When the flock continued to move in their direction, the cranes spread their huge wings in a protective shield, persuading the flock to change its direction. Following pages: The elusive snow leopard is the true predator of the heights. Its rosettes of grey on a furry creamish coat gives it perfect camouflaging among rocks and snow.

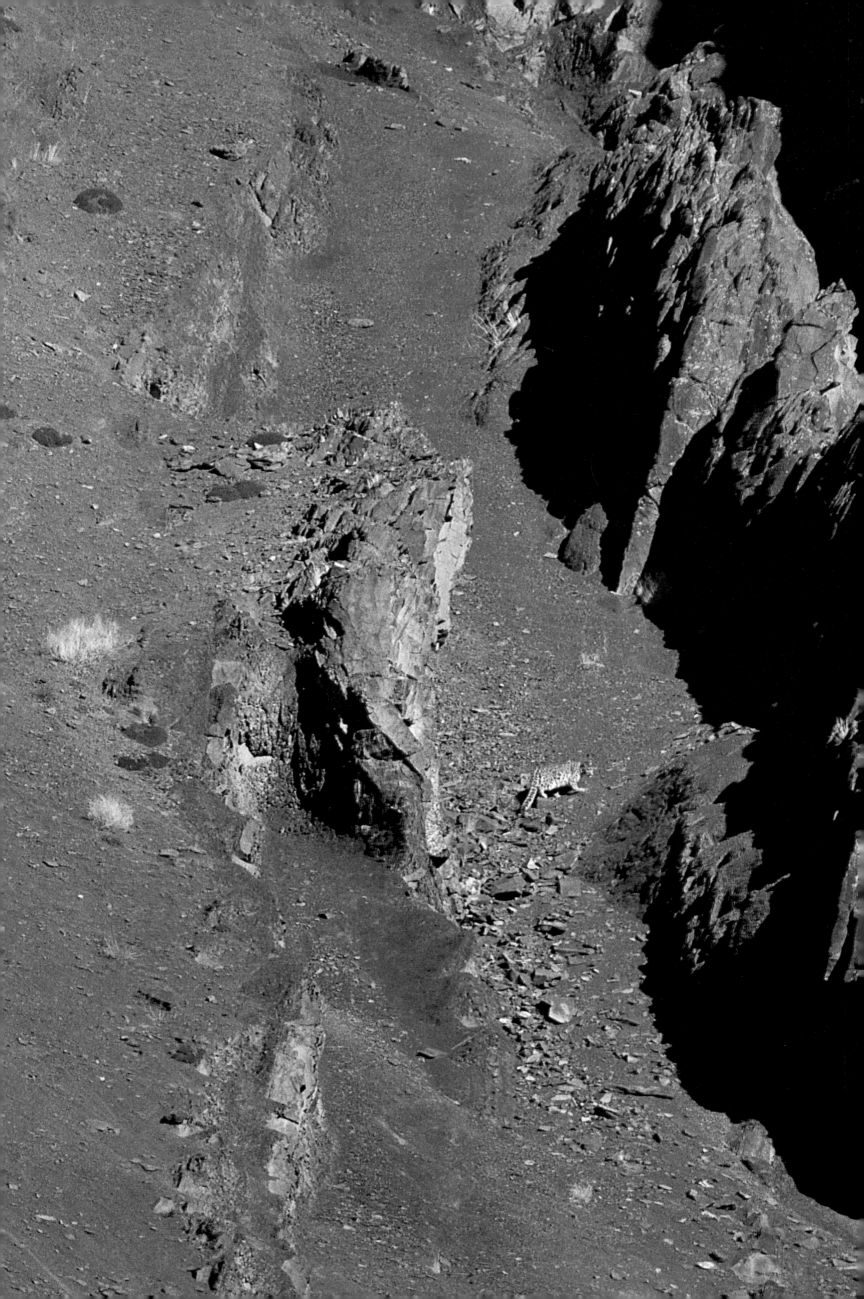

Rarely seen, the black wolf also runs with the packs in Ladakh. Wolves cover
vast territories and are hunted, in turn, by shepherds who consider them to be
dangerous pests. Preceding pages: The musk deer is a lissome high
altitude ungulate, classified between deer and antelopes. It has no antlers.
Instead, well developed canines are visible below the jaw.

Above: Neither goat nor sheep, the *bharal*, or blue sheep,
has the physical characteristics and habits of both. It can climb craggy mountain
slopes like the goat and it also enjoys feeding in open pastures like sheep. It is a
natural prey for snow leopards, wolves and the Tibetan wild dog.

The occurance of *farra*, the Tibetan wild dog, in Ladakh is not known to many people, and our unique observations on their social organisation and calls (like the bark of domestic dogs) suggest that the animal may be different from the pensular Indian wild dog. It inhabits few of the valleys and has not been seen even by many Ladakhis. The *farra* move in small packs of two or three, inhabit high elevations and prey on wild goats and sheep. The male is distinguished by a prominent mane-like ring of fur. We saw this pair kill a domestic goat by choking the trachea. Left: The hairy, black *farra* pup suckles peacefully on the rock above the den, while its wary mother stares at the photographer's hide.

The Asian wild ass in India is found in small numbers,
of around 1000. They occur in the saline desert of the little Rann
of Kutch, Gujarat, and the arctic-desert of Ladakh.
They are extremely endangered and protected by law.
Right: Some naturalists believe that *kiang*, the Tibetan
wild ass, are a distinct species. They are bigger, darker coloured
and have a thicker coat than the wild ass of the Rann of Kutch.
Kiang are well adapted for the severe winter.
They can run at high speed over the plateaus and even wolves
find it difficult to hunt them down. However, Ladakhis believe that
in neighbouring Tibet, *kiang* meat is still eaten as a delicacy.

120

The Nilgiri tahr is closely related to the Himalayan species. Now found only
in the hill ranges of south India, where it is often seen cn scarps and crags.
Large herds congregate in the uplands. Their habitat is shrinking due to increasing
tea plantations and because the meat of tahr kids is considered a
delicacy. Also known as the Nilgiri ibex.

Red panda, or the cat-bear, lives in the temperate forests of
Sikkim and Nepal above 1700 m. Nocturnal shy and solitary by nature,
spends the day curled up on a tree. They feed on bamboo shoots,
fruits, acorns, roots and sometimes small animals as well.
Adults meet only in the mating season.

Sarus cranes and blackbucks are the theme of many famous
Indian miniature paintings. Both feature prominently in the country's
religious and art history. Its striking colour and the beautifully spiralled horns
give it an elegant look. Unmatched among antelopes.
It is, perhaps, the most beautiful of antelopes.

Demoiselle cranes migrate in thousands during winter season.
They do considerable damage to crops. In Bishnoi village in Rajasthan, I have seen
big congregation sharing the village pond with cattle and villagers.

The swamp deer, mating at the Kanha National Park. Mating takes place in winter when
the forests echo with the bugling of males, who display grass masses or vegetation on their antlers.
After the adult stags leave, young males will try to playfully mount the females.

This cream coloured langur inhabits a small strip of forest close to the Manas
tiger reserve on the India-Bhutan border. The tea planter-naturalist E.P.Gee first
came up with proper evidence of the golden langur, later named *Presbytis geei*. Its hair
look golden in the winter light. Highly arboreal. they descend to the ground
only to drink water. They are exclusively vegetarian. Right: The bonnet macaque is
a pale-faced monkey common in south India. Troops of 20 to 30 can often be seen near
human settlements, without showing any fear of man. They have a highly
developed social organisation, headed by a dominant male.

A couple in courtship at the Gir sanctuary. Gir lions have
been seen mating in October and November. The thinner mane
and the drooping skin below the abdomen identifies the
Asiatic lion from its African cousin.
Right: A sub-adult lying lazily on its back after a full meal.
Unable to hunt themselves, the cubs depend on the pride for
food which is usually procured by females.
Lions are the most social of big cats.

The lion mates promiscuously with any lioness it finds
in the oestrous state. The male frequently moans and roars during
climax. Copulation is frequent and continues at
intervals for as long as a week.

In Gir, lions prey mainly on cattle, but the pride may sometimes co-ordinate
their efforts to kill camels belonging to the Maldhari cattle- breeders living inside the reserve.
An exhausted young lion relaxes, as it guards the kill for the evening feast. Overleaf: A pride going out
in search of prey at dusk. Rajesh observed a star in line with the moon, through his viewfinder,
and decided to wait for the lions to cross a particular spot. He used a handy wide angle
lens, without which this dramatic composition would not have been possible.

A flying squirrel which is a nocturnal animal, leaves its tree-hole at dusk to
feed on nearby trees. The squirrel swiftly glides from a high position on a tree to lower
heights, with aid of the thin membrane attached to its limbs. When it leaps into the air the outstretched
limbs expand the membrane to the fullest, creating a parachute effect. Following pages:
An elephant herd at sunset in Corbett National Park.